# MAKE MONEY FROM MAKES

A guide to turning your hobby into a business

by Emma Jones

**prima**

**brightword**

A Brightword book | **www.brightwordpublishing.com**

HARRIMAN HOUSE LTD
3A Penns Road
Petersfield
Hampshire
GU32 2EW
GREAT BRITAIN

Tel: +44 (0)1730 233870 | Fax: +44 (0)1730 233880
Email: enquiries@harriman-house.com | Website: **www.harriman-house.com**

ISBN: 9781908003485

British Library Cataloguing in Publication Data | A CIP catalogue record for this book can be obtained from the British
Library.

Printed and bound in the UK by CPI Group (UK) Ltd, Croydon, CR0 4YY
Set in Minion and Sanchez

# CONTENTS

Emma Jones

# ABOUT THE AUTHOR

EMMA JONES is a business expert, author and founder of small business community Enterprise Nation. Her books include *Spare Room Start Up*, *Working 5 to 9*, *Go Global* and *The Start-Up Kit.*

Following a five-year career at an international accounting firm, Emma started her first business at 27. That business was sold 18 months later, and the experience led to Emma's next venture, Enterprise Nation. Its website was launched in 2006 and became the most popular for home business owners in the UK, attracting over 100,000 visitors each month.

The site and business has grown into a friendly community of over 75,000 small business owners who help each other and benefit from the knowledge of experts through Enterprise Nation blogs, guides, books, eBooks, apps, kits and events.

Emma is also a co-founder of national campaign StartUp Britain, and received an MBE for services to enterprise in June 2012.

@emmaljones | www.enterprisenation.com

# Get the eBook of

# MAKE MONEY
# FROM MAKES

## for free

*As a buyer of the printed version of this book you can download the eBook version free of charge in formats compatible with Kindle, iPad, Kobo and other eBook readers. Just point your tablet or camera phone at the code above or go to:*

**ebooks.harriman-house.com/makes**

# FOREWORD

**W**HEN *Prima* launched back in October 1986, we promised to bring our readers '*knitting, embroidery, handicrafts, sewing and all kinds of makes*' in every single issue, and our front cover screamed '*Fun, fast and creative: Crafts you'll love to do!*' Not much has changed in 26 years – you're still a crafty bunch – and from the hundreds of letters we receive each month, we know that craft inspiration is just as relevant to you today as it was in the eighties. For many of our readers, crafting is a way of escaping the treadmill of daily life, for others it's relaxing to have an absorbing project after a mentally taxing day and for all it's about the simple pride and pleasure that comes from creating something from scratch.

Some things of course *have* changed over the past couple of decades – more women than ever work full time, and our lives are busier than before. More often than not, me-time languishes at the bottom of our list of priorities, somewhere in between

 For many, crafting is a way of escaping – for others it's relaxing."

filing your phone bill and de-cluttering the cupboards. So wouldn't it be great if you could do a little of what you love every day, and make a living at the same time, bringing better balance to your life? By picking up a copy of this informative and inspiring book, you've already taken the first step towards turning your talent into turnover, and making a profit from your passion!

The way we shop has transformed in recent years – with such a wealth of consumer products to pick from at the touch of a button, we're increasingly demanding unique, one-off items for ourselves, our children, or to give as gifts. People are starting to take more notice of where and how products are made. It seems we've come full circle and adopted some of the thinking of our foremothers, with a make-do-and-mend mindset and a distaste for our throwaway society – our *Prima* readers have always been canny consumers as well as clever crafters! The UK handmade market is enjoying a real renaissance, and there's never been a better time to become part of the crafting community.

So if you're a producer of handmade products and wondering whether you could turn your hobby into a business; where to sell your products; how to price them; and how to build a brand, we're here to show you how – in the no-nonsense way you'd expect from *Prima*. It's jam-packed with top hints and tips and will guide you step by step through the process, with real-life inspiration from people who have already made the leap – people just like you. You'll discover how to make sales, write a business plan, protect your work and promote yourself.

For most of us living in these financially fraught times, work means doing what ever it takes to pay the bills and feed the family. But by being in control of your working life and making a living from what you love, you can make 'work' feel a lot like play.

With the technology at our fingertips, we're no longer fettered by expensive start-up costs or the uncertainty of ditching the day job – people are rapidly realising that you can start a business in your spare time and from the comfort of your own home, often for less than £100! And the freedom and flexibility that comes from being able to choose when, where and how you work is *priceless*.

With clear steps, useful links and expert advice, we hope you'll find this book an invaluable craft companion as you turn your talent into a business – whether that's card-making at your kitchen table or sewing from your sofa!

We'd love to hear about your journey as you learn to *Make Money From Makes*.

*Maire Fahey*

Editor, *Prima* Magazine

Tell us about your business by posting what you're all about and some pics on *Prima* Magazine's Facebook wall at **www.facebook.com/primamagazine** and contacting via Twitter **@PrimaMag**.

# INTRODUCTION

A N increasing number of people are turning their passion, hobby or skill into a way of making a living, and you could be one of them! In 2011, a record half a million people started their own business and are enjoying the freedom and flexibility that comes with being their own boss.

It's now perfectly possible to start a business whilst holding down a job (I refer to it as Working 5 to 9!) and to start on a bootstrap of a budget.

Every day I hear from business owners who are operating from home and embracing free or low-cost technology to source, make and promote their products and services. They are keeping costs low but are big on ambition. Of the 16 businesses profiled in this book, 63% of them are also going global and selling all over the world.

All you need is an idea, a commitment to make sales, knowledge of how to make some noise and you're in business! In this book I'll show you how it's done and offer links to many organisations and websites that have been set up to help and support you.

From funding to social media, technology and sales, there's advice all around; it's on offer from the government, from private sector campaigns such as StartUp Britain and from small business websites such as my own, and others.

I hope you enjoy this book and make the most of the support available to start and grow your business. Please keep in touch to let me know how your journey is developing and I look forward to profiling you on our website or in future eBooks and books!

Emma Jones

**emma@enterprisenation.com | @emmaljones**

# WHO IS THIS BOOK FOR?

THIS book is for anyone who has a passion, skill or hobby and an interest in turning this into a business. You may be baking cakes for friends and family and dreaming of doing this full time, or have a way with words that could be turned into commissions. Maybe you paint or draw and wonder if those who offer praise would be prepared to pay for your creations, or whether your flair for fashion could lead to financial return.

Whatever your talent, it's likely you can turn this into a business with customers paying for the quality products you offer. Whether artisan or tailor, writer or baker, what you will discover from this book is how to:

- Make sales beyond friends and family

- Promote your brand and become well known

- Register the company and manage the finances

- Embrace technology to save time and money

- Convey a professional image; online and off

- Create a support network and work with partners

Above all, it shows how to make money from doing what you love!

The book is divided into clear chapters with stories throughout of people who have successfully started and grown their own business; from Laura Helps who started out making cakes and is now building a business around helping others do the same, to Sandra Lewis who left a 20-year corporate career to develop a global VA business, and mother and daughter team Marion Paterson and Emily McIntyre who have turned misfortune into a thriving venture that sells handmade jewellery to customers both locally and further afield. They all offer their stories and top tips for success.

With clear steps, useful links and expert advice, consider this book your guide as you turn talent into a business, and share it with friends and family who are doing the same!

# CONTRIBUTORS

With thanks to the following people who have contributed their expertise or story in the compilation of this book …

## MONEY MAKERS

Ellie Barwick – Truly Treats

Victoria Cramsie – PaperBoy Interiors

Susan Elena – DanceHQ

Marion Paterson and Emily McIntyre – Ruby and Rose Jewellery

Sarah Cuthbertson – Just Brownies

Emma Maudsley – Sock Monkey Emporium

Lucy Lee – Lily Charmed

Maggie Conway – Robin and Rose

Charity Nichols – Green Tulip

Amanda Frolich – Amanda's Action Club

Denise Rawls – Strange Fruit Greeting Cards

Julie Dodsworth – Julie Dodsworth Designs

Laura Helps – Cakes by Laura

Sandra Lewis – Worldwide101

Joanna Michaelides – Just Puddings

Denise Charlesworth-Smith – Crystal Pig Accessories

## EXPERTS

Joanne Dewberry – Charlie Moo's

Cally Robson – She's Ingenious

Patrick Lockton – Matrix Law Group

Emily Coltman – FreeAgent

Laura Rigney – Pitcher House

Dan Wilson – Tamebay

Jackie Wade – Winning Sales

Greg Simpson – Press For Attention

San Sharma – Enterprise Nation

## PRIMA MAGAZINE CONTRIBUTORS

Mel Hunter

# CHAPTER ONE
## COMING UP WITH AN IDEA

**W**HEN starting a business, the first step is to come up with an idea for what the business will do and on which of your skills it will be based. Many talented people tell me their problem is not coming up with one idea, it's a case of having too many ideas! In response, my advice is to spend time working on them all but focus on the product that sells, i.e. let the market dictate the idea that becomes the core of your business.

Throughout, bear in mind that a niche business is often the best kind of business.

## NICHE IS NICE

Niche is nice! What I mean by this is: craft your hobby, passion or skill so it becomes a product that meets the needs of a well-defined audience.

There are two key benefits to having a niche business:

**1.** You keep marketing costs low, as your audience is well defined; you know where your audience are and you have researched and understand the kind of marketing messages to which they will respond.

**2.** Customer loyalty remains high, as you become the expert in your field or the only provider of certain products, thereby encouraging customers to return and buy from you to benefit from the specialist product you offer.

Think about how you can fashion your talent into an idea that has a clear purpose for a clearly defined audience.

This book shows you how to base a business on what you enjoy doing, whilst at the same time having an eye on what people will buy. Ellie Barwick discovered there was a market for her products after attending car boot sales and farmers' markets . . .

# MONEY MAKER

**NAME**: Ellie Barwick

**TALENT**: Baking

**BUSINESS**: Truly Treats

ELLIE BARWICK's business, Truly Treats, began after a winter season spent working in a chalet in France with her partner Adam.

"We had to cook a full breakfast for our 14 guests every day, a four-course evening meal and we also had to bake a cake each day. We received so many compliments about our cooking, in particular our cakes, that we returned to the UK in March 2010 and wondered if this was something we could turn into a business."

Ellie started out by attending car boot sales and local farmers' markets as she was keen to get her products out there for people to see and taste. She was thrilled when

people began to snap them up: "It's amazing how quickly the word spreads when you have a great product."

From there, Truly Treats has grown from a business started at the kitchen table to a dedicated commercial unit in Teignmouth.

4

"The first two years were spent working from home, just the two of us, and occasionally drafting in family members or friends when things got a bit hectic. We now have my brother working for us full time. We really wanted our first employee to be someone we could trust 100% and that we knew wouldn't let us down. It's working really well so far."

Truly Treats now supplies cafés, restaurants, hotels, tearooms and farm shops in South Devon and Ellie is keen to expand on this in the future.

Ellie has found social media a great way to keep her customers up to date with what's going on in the business. She's also found local magazine and newspapers to be an effective source of promotion, as well as attending a range of food events and fairs throughout Devon.

"We've found that putting ourselves in front of the public is a great way to promote what we do."

Ellie and Adam have big plans for Truly Treats and are working on expanding their wholesale customer base throughout Devon. It's an exciting time for this entrepreneurial couple!

**TOP TIP!** *"Never give up – even when you feel like you're going mad! Stay committed and try to stay strong. The rewards are really worth it in the end."*

❀ **www.trulytreats.com**

❀ **www.facebook.com/TrulyTreats**

❀ **@Truly_Treats**

# RESEARCHING THE MARKET

Research your potential customers, the competition and price points by visiting competitors' sites, online trade sites/forums, reading reports, and seeking intelligence from experts. Look for information that will answer the following questions:

❀ What is the number of potential customers you can serve, and how do these customers like to be served?

❀ What are their characteristics, spending patterns and who are their key influencers?

❀ Who is currently serving your market?

❀ Where are your potential customers going for their goods?

❀ What do they like about what they're getting and, more importantly, what do they dislike (as this opens up opportunities for you to improve on the status quo)?

In view of the above, is there a business here? Is there room in the market for your business and is the demand there? If so, think about what price you could charge for your product.

Price yourself at a rate that's competitive with other providers in the market, that takes into account the amount of time, personal service and added value you offer, and that will turn a profit at the end of the day!

# RESEARCH TOOLS

To find answers to your questions and to source information on competitors, visit forums and sites where your potential customers gather and read up on the local competition. Get on Google, follow links posted on social media sites such as Facebook and Twitter, and find out who's out there and what people are saying about them.

Visit competitor websites, and consider buying from them to get an idea of their strong points – and maybe their weaknesses too – so that when you come to set up your business, you know what you like and what you don't like!

## Social media channels

- Twitter | **www.twitter.com**
- Facebook | **www.facebook.com**
- LinkedIn | **www.linkedin.com**

Carry out research face-to-face by displaying goods at fairs and markets and complete the market research template below to be sure there's a sufficient market of people to buy your products at a price that will turn a profit.

- How big is the market?
- What is the number of potential customers I can serve and how do these customers like to be served?
- What are their characteristics, spending patterns and who are their key influencers?
- Who is currently serving my market?
- Where are my potential customers currently going for their goods?

❀ What do they like about what they're getting and, more importantly, what do they dislike?

❀ What price can I charge for my products? What's competitive and takes into account the amount of time, personal service and added value that I offer?

More information on producing and pricing your products can be found from page 67, and details on how to create a basic cash flow sheet are on page 66.

## FRIENDS AND FAMILY FOCUS GROUP

When moving from hobby to business, friends and family represent a key focus group and your most ardent supporters. Talk through your ideas and ask for feedback on the product itself and your qualities in being able to deliver. Conversations with friends and family will help you prepare an initial SWOT analysis for the business.

## SWOT ANALYSIS

With your idea and research in hand, prepare a SWOT analysis. This stands for: **S**trengths, **W**eaknesses, **O**pportunities, **T**hreats.

## **S**TRENGTHS

*What are my strengths?*
*What can I do better than anyone else?*
*What resources do I have?*
*What's my unique selling point?*

## **W**EAKNESSES

*What are my weaknesses?*
*What should I avoid?*
*Where do I lack skills?*
*What might hinder my success?*

## **O**PPORTUNITIES

*What opportunities do I see?*
*Does my idea tap into any trends?*
*Are there any emerging technologies that*
*could help my idea?*
*Has there been anything in the news related to*
*my idea?*

## **T**HREATS

*What threats would I face?*
*Who's my competition?*
*Does changing technology affect my*
*idea?*

# THE NAME GAME

Coming up with an idea and carrying out research will get you thinking about what to name your new baby (by which I mean your business!).

A good start is to think of a name that:

❀ is easy to spell

❀ is not already registered with Companies House (you can use a free webcheck service to access existing company names at **www.companieshouse.gov.uk**) or trademarked

❀ people will remember

❀ has an available domain name.

You might want to protect the name with a trademark to make sure that no one else can use it in the future. See page 36 for more information.

If you get stuck, visit Enterprise Nation (**www.enterprisenation.com**) where you will find people who can help you win the name game, as the site is buzzing with talented copywriters and wordsmiths.

Victoria Cramsie's business was not named after her two young sons but it was in trying to buy something for them that caused her to spot a gap in the market . . .

# MONEY MAKER

**NAME**: Victoria Cramsie

**TALENT**: Handmade Craft/Design

**BUSINESS**: PaperBoy Interiors

VICTORIA CRAMSIE's business, PaperBoy, was conceived when her two six-year-old boys, Rory and Archie, outgrew their nursery-style room and needed a place that they (and Victoria) could be proud of.

She started to look for boy's wallpaper that wasn't folksy or twee, but kept coming up against tacky, standard, licensed wallpaper that didn't fit her or her boys' style. "There's nothing in the world for boys that's nice," Victoria says, "so I gave up looking and got making."

Victoria was always a fan of the handmade look so began to work on some images, drawing on research from her boys and their friends.

> "They liked 'edgy' images, from graffiti to slightly scary skeletons, and more classic images like pets, puppets and dinosaurs. And they responded in a surprisingly sophisticated way to colour, simplicity and texture."

She came up with designs that would appeal to boys from pre-school to teens, something for after the fluffy bunny stage that would see them through until they paint their bedrooms black!

PaperBoy's first customer came through NotOnTheHighStreet.com, a platform site for artisans to sell their goods. "The first thing I ever sold was a sample of the 'D'ya-

think-e-saurus' wallpaper in green and red," Victoria recalls, and from there she has taken her business global.

"We now ship internationally via the PaperBoy website and we also have stockists around the world, from Russia to Australia and Germany. The internet has made global trading very straightforward for us."

Editorial features in the press have been a powerful way for Victoria to promote the business.

"I was really lucky in the early stages to have been picked up by some quite powerful design blogs and this then lead on to print editorial. I now use a PR company who deal with all the image and press requests for the business, but for the first two years it was just me."

PaperBoy uses Twitter to keep in touch with customers and to connect customers with the brand.

"We aim to always give great customer service and make a unique and interesting product. We get a lot of repeat trade customers (interior designers) so I take from this that the product and service is up to scratch."

Although Victoria works mostly on her own, she has grown the business through outsourcing and using freelance workers.

"I use other people more and more – for example the PR company now works on a full-time basis – and I also employ freelancers for marketing campaigns and sending out samples and orders when we're really busy. Employing people on a freelance basis allows me the freedom to call on people when needed."

This approach means Victoria can grow PaperBoy without worrying about the costs of moving into premises or the pricey overheads of fixed salaries, but can pull in extra and expert resource when the business is at its busiest.

Victoria plans to continue to grow the business over the next couple of years and explore other areas into which the brand can expand.

**TOP TIP!** *"Be sure you have a unique and well made product. But most of all make sure that there is actually a market for it."*

❀ **www.paperboywallpaper.co.uk**

❀ **www.facebook.com/PaperBoyWallpaper**

❀ **@PaperBoyLondon**

# 6 TIPS FOR LAUNCHING YOUR CRAFT BUSINESS

JOANNE DEWBERRY, founder of Charlie Moo's (**www.charliemoos.co.uk**) and author of *Crafting a Successful Small Business* (**www.enterprisenation.com/shop**) provides her top tips for launching your craft business . . .

**1.** Start with something you know (you can develop other skills behind the scenes). This way you can be confident and know the products are of a suitable quality.

**2.** Decide where you will sell, whether that's on or offline, craft fairs and/or websites.

**3.** Research what others are making, where they sell, the prices they sell at and how they are branded and marketed. Find out if you need any information on your products' packaging. Do they need testing? Do you need any certification? Food or natural products will need ingredients listing, kitchens will need to be inspected by environmental health, toys will need CE testing for health and safety, etc. Make sure you know what's required.

**4.** Pricing is vital. You have to take everything into consideration; factor in waste, shipping, equipment, advertising, utilities such as the internet, electricity, telephones, time and your hourly wage.

**5.** Test the market. Get your products in front of others. Find out what they like – and don't like. Talk to family members, but they are normally well meaning and may not provide the helpful criticism you need, so test your products on strangers too – a market is a good starting place.

**6.** Have fun – that's why you started in the first place!

# CHAPTER TWO
## I'M OFF

# BUSINESS PLAN

FTER coming up with your product idea and doing your research, writing a brief business plan is your first practical step to starting your business. With it under your belt you can say, "I'm off!"

A business plan will act as your map; it will guide the business from start to growth, with reference to milestones along the way. For example, you might want to open a shop, launch a website or reach a number of customers within a certain time frame.

The plan will include information about how you intend to get started and what your ultimate objectives are – and how you aim to get from one to the other. You might want to start a business and sell it in a few years' time, or grow to a point where you wouldn't want to grow anymore. And, of course, you'll need to refer to resources: what you have already, what you'll need and how you'll pay for it.

You may also need a plan if you're looking to raise money, from friends or family or from the bank.

With it in hand, you'll be off on your business journey. Or IMOFF.

It's an easy way to remember the headings to include in your business plan:

- ❀ **I**dea
- ❀ **M**arket
- ❀ **O**perations
- ❀ **F**inancials
- ❀ **F**riends

# **I**DEA
*What's your idea?*

# **M**ARKET
*Who will be your customers or clients? And who is your competition?*

# **O**PERATIONS
*How will you develop the idea, promote it, and provide good customer service?*

# **F**INANCIALS
*Can you earn more than you spend, so that the business makes a profit? Do you need any funds to get started?*

# **F**RIENDS
*Do you have a support network on hand for when you need business advice? Are there complementary businesses you've identified with whom partnerships are a possibility?*

Have these as headings in your plan and you've taken a big step closer to becoming your own boss.

## TIP: REVISIT REGULARLY

*Review your plan regularly to check progress against targets or to make amends as you respond to new opportunities. I revisit the Enterprise Nation plan for a 'gentle' recap every six months and then at the start of each year head off for a couple of days to re-read the plan, rethink the business, and rewrite if required.*

# BUSINESS PLAN TEMPLATE

Use this template to write your own business plan.

**Executive Summary**

......................................................................................

**The Idea**

......................................................................................

**The Market**
Customers

......................................................................................

Competition

......................................................................................

**Operations**
CEO

......................................................................................

Sourcing

......................................................................................

**Sales & Marketing**
Press

......................................................................................

Online

......................................................................................

Partners

......................................................................................

Systems

......................................................................................

**Friends & Family**

......................................................................................

# MONEY MAKER

**NAME**: Susan Elena

**TALENT**: Dancing

**BUSINESS**: Dance HQ

SUSAN ELENA had always dreamt about starting up a dance company but wanted to make the most of the travelling opportunities a freelance dancer is given before settling in one place. At the start of 2010, after an eight-year freelance career teaching, choreographing and performing both nationally and internationally, she felt like it was the right time to move to a more permanent base, and as she spent most of her time driving to various school gym halls she knew there was a gap in the market for a proper dance studio.

> "My mum, an accountant and my business partner, and I combined our strengths to search for the right premises. In July 2010 we signed the lease on three units in Glasgow's historic Templeton Carpet Factory which we then spent three months converting into two large dance studios and a spacious, central reception area. Dance HQ opened its doors in September 2010."

Susan was lucky to have a database of potential clients through her freelance work, including people she'd already been teaching in various different venues in Glasgow and the surrounding areas, who were all able to come to her classes at her new central location and get the business up and running.

> "I tried to keep the classes they had been attending at the same time during the week to make it as easy as possible for them to come along, and because I was able to offer many more dance styles than I could on my own, I was able to attract new customers.

The freelance tutors who taught classes at Dance HQ were all encouraged to involve their own clients as well which meant that word spread quite quickly."

Dance HQ promote themselves through a very strong online presence with Facebook, Twitter, Instagram, LinkedIn, Google+ and YouTube profiles, plus their own website that is updated regularly, a blog featuring a range of dance-related articles and a fortnightly newsletter sent out to their mailing list.

"Our clients are primarily female aged 18-40 and they spend a lot of time on social networking sites so we ensure that our online voice reflects our real-life image."

Susan has also decided to use posters, banners and flyers posted around the city in or near venues which attract their main demographic and they also regularly turn up to theatre or music events to hand out flyers.

"Last year we surprised Glasgow's shoppers with a flash mob on Buchanan Street, also known as the Style Mile, which then led to other companies requesting their own flash mobs."

The Dance HQ studios have also attracted numerous high-profile events and dancers including Anton Du Beke and Erin Boag who trained the Miss Scotland finalists and Brendan Cole and Jo Wood on their recent Flora Pro-Activ Swing into Dance tour, who have all commented positively on the image, facilities and professionalism of the company: "This positive feedback from some of the world's most recognised dancers is fantastic promotion for us."

To keep customers coming back time and time again, Dance HQ's tutors always tell their classes what will be happening the following week and also try to greet each client by name and make time to chat to everyone before or after class.

"When customers feel valued they begin to feel like part of the team and want to come back for more. We also offer monthly deals as a special thank you to our customers. Having tried an online group discount site with disappointing results we decided to take that idea and make it our own. Every month we offer a limited number of monthly deals which give our customers great discounts without the financial risk to us as a business, it's a win-win situation."

Dance HQ has two directors; one of whom is full-time and deals with all of the dance work and day-to-day running of the studios, and the other who still works full-time for another company and spends evenings and weekends dealing with the financial side of the business.

"Initially we operated with a team of freelancers who each came in and taught a few classes per week but in January 2012 we employed our first part-time dance tutor who was able to take on more classes each week and have more involvement in the company's development. We still have a couple of freelancers who teach specialist classes so the team is small but tightly knit."

Susan does have plans to branch out but this is more likely to be nationally first before internationally. However, Dance HQ have already welcomed dancers from Europe, the USA and Australia to their studios so, for now, they're happy with the world coming to them!

Dance HQ is only two years old so Susan feels that the next twelve months will be crucial in building upon their foundations.

"We'd love to expand and open up new studios in the future but the coming year is all about continuing to offer a wide range of classes to people of all ages, providing stunning rehearsal space for visiting companies and developing our education and outreach programme. We have plans to develop a professional dance troupe for events and hope to be involved in the Glasgow 2014 celebrations which are due to start being developed in the coming year. Our aim is to be the best at what we do, get a really strong foundation in place and learn from our mistakes before we expand to other venues."

**TOP TIP!** *"Start as you mean to go on! Get everything in place before you launch your business and have an idea about what you want to represent and offer your clients but be flexible enough to change things that don't work and be open to new ideas. Dance Hen Parties weren't part of our original business plan but are now one of our biggest sources of revenue. The thing that hasn't changed is our professionalism, quality and image and these are the things that people will remember."*

❀ **www.dancehq.co.uk**

❀ **www.facebook.com/DanceHQ**

❀ **@Dance_HQ**

# CHAPTER THREE
## THE MUST-DO'S

**A**s the business comes into being, so does a duty to register the company as a trading entity. There's also the company assets to consider (brand/name/idea) and how to protect them.

# REGISTER THE COMPANY

When you set up in business there is one key organisation to contact and inform: HM Revenue & Customs (HMRC). You may also need to register with Companies House. Before contacting either, have a think about the company status that suits you best. There are a number of options:

## SELF-EMPLOYED

As it sounds, this means working for yourself; you keep records and accounts of your own activity, and, in acting alone, get to keep all the profits – but are also solely liable for any debts.

If you set up as a self-employed sole trader you don't need to register with Companies House or take on any of the accounting duties that come with being a limited company, as outlined below.

## PARTNERSHIP

If you'd like to be self-employed but want to work with a friend or colleague, consider a partnership. It means that two or more people share the risks, costs, profits and workload. Partnerships do not have to file accounts at Companies House but there are filing requirements with HM Revenue & Customs, as outlined below.

A limited liability partnership or LLP is structured in the same way as a normal partnership but, as it sounds, limits the liability of each partner. An LLP has the same filing requirements at Companies House as a limited company.

Find out more about the legal status of partnerships on the Business Link site at: **tinyurl.com/6k7dmml**

# LIMITED COMPANY

Limited companies exist in their own right, with the company's finances kept separate from the personal finances of its owner(s). Limited companies have filing responsibilities with both Companies House and HMRC as noted below but it's now much easier to launch a limited company as there is no longer a need to appoint a company secretary. You can be a limited company with a headcount of one, which many small businesses are!

The status of your company will affect how much admin you have to do and the kind of financial records you must keep and file. Take advice from your accountant or local tax office on which one to choose as much depends on the type of business you will be running.

## TIP: BEING SOCIAL

*Should you decide to start a social enterprise – a business trading for social and environmental purposes – there are additional legal structures to consider, including:*

❀ *community interest company (CIC)*

❀ *industrial and provident society*

❀ *charitable status.*

*To find out more about launching a social enterprise or creating a community interest company (CIC) visit:*

❀ *Social Enterprise UK* | **www.socialenterprise.org.uk**

❀ *CIC Regulator* | **www.cicregulator.gov.uk**

# COMPANIES HOUSE

When registering with Companies House there are two options from which to choose. You can buy a 'ready-made' company from a company formation agent, or 'incorporate' a company yourself by sending documents and a registration fee to Companies House. If you decide to complete registration yourself, download the form from **bit.ly/ezw1S**.

# COSTS

### Self-incorporation

Visit the new company registration page of the Companies House website (**bit.ly/dw1xcJ**), complete form IN01 and post it to Companies House along with the relevant fee:

❀ Standard service fee is £20 (documents processed in eight to ten days).

❀ Same-day service fee is £50.

## Company formation agent

Prices start at £25 for standard company registration. Try websites such as:

- ✿ The Company Warehouse | **www.thecompanywarehouse.co.uk**
- ✿ Jordans | **www.jordans.co.uk**
- ✿ Companies Made Simple | **www.companiesmadesimple.com**
- ✿ UK Plc | **www.uk-plc.net**

# HM REVENUE & CUSTOMS

The rules on registering a new business with HM Revenue & Customs are pretty clear-cut. You are required to register as soon as you start earning from any business activity. As above, you can choose to register as self-employed, as a partnership, or as a limited company. Each category has its own filing requirements, as outlined below.

# SOLE TRADER/SELF-EMPLOYED

The calculation of tax due and National Insurance owing is done through self-assessment.

You either need to complete form CWF1 or call the newly self-employed business helpline. This should be done within three months of undertaking your first piece of self-employed work in order to avoid a fine.

- ✿ Form CWF1 | **www.hmrc.gov.uk/forms/cwf1.pdf**
- ✿ Helpline for the newly self-employed | 0845 915 4515

It's not onerous to complete the form, and once registered you'll be classified as self-employed and sent a self-assessment tax return each year, which you complete, showing your income and expenses from self-employment as well as details of your employment elsewhere (if applicable).

You will be subject to tax and National Insurance on any profits you make, but the good news is that any losses incurred can be offset against your employed income (if you have any), which could even result in a tax rebate.

Depending on your turnover and how straightforward your tax affairs are, you may be able to complete the Short Tax Return (SA200). However, this cannot be self-selected, nor is it on the HMRC website or orderable; HMRC will send it to you automatically if they think you qualify, based on information given in the previous year's return. If you have turnover below £68,000, it's likely that you will qualify. As ever, though, it will depend on individual circumstances, and the law (and various criteria it uses) may change!

### Deadlines

Self-assessment tax return deadlines are as follows:

❀ Paper tax returns should be received by HMRC by 31 October of tax year ending 5 April.

❀ Online tax returns should be completed by 31 January (giving you an extra three months).

---

**TIP: USEFUL LINKS**

*Leaflet SE1 – 'Thinking of working for yourself?'* | **www.hmrc.gov.uk/leaflets/se1.pdf**

*Helping you understand self-assessment and your tax return* | **www.hmrc.gov.uk/sa**

---

# PARTNERSHIP

According to HMRC, a partnership is where:

> "Two or more people set up a business. Each partner is personally responsible for all the business debts, even if the debt was caused by another partner. As partners, each pays income tax on their share of the business profits through self-assessment, as well as National Insurance."

In terms of filing requirements, each partner should complete a partnership supplementary page as part of their individual self-assessment tax return. This is in addition to a partnership return, which has to be submitted by one nominated partner and show each partner's share of profits/losses.

## Deadlines

The deadlines for partnership tax returns are as follows:

❀ Paper tax returns should be received by HMRC by 31 October of tax year ending 5 April.

❀ Online tax returns should be completed by 31 January (giving you an extra three months).

See page 174 for guidance on how to write a partnership agreement.

# LIMITED COMPANY

As mentioned, limited company's finances are distinct from the finances of their owner(s). What this means is that the company is liable for its own debts, not the individual owners, as is the case if you are self-employed or in a partnership. In April 2008 it became legal to form and run a limited company with just one person, without the need to involve anyone else (prior to this, by law you also needed a company secretary).

As mentioned earlier, you can form a new limited company by registering with Companies House (**www.companieshouse.gov.uk**) or by using a company creation agent.

As well as registering with Companies House, you also need to let HMRC know you are operating as a limited company. You can do this by completing form CT41G.

You will also need to set up and register a PAYE scheme as you are an employee of the company.

- Register PAYE scheme | **www.hmrc.gov.uk/newemployers**
- New employer's helpline | 0845 60 70 143

In terms of filing requirements, you must complete a self-assessment company tax return at the end of the accounting period. The return will show the company's taxable profits and whether any corporation tax is owed, and can be filed online at **www.hmrc.gov.uk/ct**. The return should also be filed with Companies House to comply with the Companies Act 2006. This can be done free of charge, using their online WebFiling: **ewf.companieshouse.gov.uk**

On your returns, you can claim wear-and-tear allowances (capital allowances) on any work-related equipment you buy, and also an element of your expenses for working from home. You can also claim travelling expenses, subsistence and a proportion of your phone calls.

Visit the 'Tax allowances and reliefs if you're self-employed' section of the Business Link website to see what you can claim: **tinyurl.com/5sjt2sx**

## Deadlines

Company tax returns must be filed within twelve months of the end of your company's corporation tax accounting period. More details on these deadlines can be found at: **www.hmrc.gov.uk/ct/deadlines**

---

**TIP: IN GOOD ORDER**

*Keep records of your business dealings – this will make it much easier to complete tax returns when the time comes. Keep hold of:*

❀ *receipts of business-related purchases*

❀ *copies of invoices to customers*

❀ *bank statements (especially if you don't have a separate account for the business; see page 77 on how to start one)*

❀ *utility bills (if you are starting the business from home and using part of the house for business); they can be claimed as a business expense and so reduce your tax bill.*

*For advice from HMRC on good record keeping, visit:* **www.hmrc.gov.uk/record-keeping**

---

# VAT

Whichever tax status you choose, if your business turns over more than £77,000 (2012/13 tax year), or you think your turnover will soon exceed this amount, you should also register for value added tax (VAT).

You can voluntarily register at any time. Being VAT-registered can bring credibility with certain customers, but adding VAT to your invoices may make you more expensive than competitors and you will have to file a VAT return four times a year.

❀ How and when to register for VAT | **www.hmrc.gov.uk/vat/start/register**

# ACCOUNTANT ACCOMPANIMENT

Talk to a qualified accountant about the structure that is best for your business. And consider employing their services to complete your tax returns. Even if your accounts are very simple, it is well worth seeking professional advice, particularly as the rules and regulations can change frequently and without warning.

Find an accountant by visiting:

- ❀ ICAEW (Institute of Chartered Accountants in England and Wales) | **www.icaew.com**

- ❀ List of Sage-accredited professionals | **www.sage.co.uk/partner**

- ❀ Accountant partners of online software tool FreeAgent | **www.freeagent.com/partners**

- ❀ Enterprise Nation has an online marketplace of business service providers | **www.enterprisenation.com**

## TIP: USEFUL LINKS

- ❀ *Starting a Business* | **www.hmrc.gov.uk/startingup**
- ❀ *Tax help and advice for small business* | **www.businesslink.gov.uk/taxhelp**

# BUSINESS RATES

The final form of tax to bear in mind is business rates. If you have applied for planning permission or your local authority is aware you are running a business from home, they may try to charge you business rates as opposed to council tax on the part of the house being used for business purposes. Business rates are different in each area and something that should be discussed with your local authority.

❀  Business Link on business rates | **www.businesslink.gov.uk/businessrates**

See page 39 to determine if you need to contact your local authority about planning permission and therefore the applicability of business rates.

# PROTECT THE BRAND

You have now registered with HM Revenue & Customs and possibly Companies House. Your final consideration should be your intellectual property. You may decide to register a trademark to protect your company name or brand or, if you've come up with a unique invention, a patent. This means that companies can't come along and use your name or invention without your permission.

## THE FOUR FORMS OF IP

There are four different kinds of intellectual property that you can protect.

### 1. Patents

These are, essentially, what makes things work. For example, says the Intellectual Property Office (IPO), "what makes a wheel turn or the chemical formula of your favourite fizzy drink".

### 2. Trademarks

These are "signs (like words and logos) that distinguish goods and services in the marketplace".

## 3. Designs

What a logo or product looks like, "from the shape of an aeroplane to a fashion item".

## 4. Copyright

An automatic right that comes into existence for anything written or recorded.

Visit the UK Intellectual Property Office website to carry out searches, register trademarks and read up on all things IP-related.

❀ Intellectual Property Office | **www.ipo.gov.uk**

We asked Cally Robson from She's Ingenious!, the Association of Women with new Products and Inventions, for her advice about getting your products registered and protected by the Intellectual Property Office:

**Q.** *Is IP protection as important whether you're delivering products or services, i.e. whether I'm selling a homemade pot or a poem, should I still consider protection?*

**A.** Yes. Whatever the nature of your business, to distinguish yourself from the competition you need to be unique in some way. IP law basically offers a way to protect what is special about your business. Although IP might feel less relevant in a service-oriented business, it is just as key. Registering a distinct logo and/or name as a trademark, buying a strong web address, and building your brand should all be part of the IP strategy for a service-based business.

**Q.** *What is the difference between patents, trademarks and copyright?*

**A.** It is important to understand the differences between forms of IP protection. There are great guides on the Intellectual Property Office website but, basically, patents protect concepts that are technically innovative, copyright gives automatic protection to anything that can be put down on a piece of paper, and trademarks protect the name and/or logo of your business. Don't forget design protection too – as well as being able to register designs, it is little known that you also have automatic protection.

**Q**. *How much will it cost to protect my idea or product?*

**A**. How long is a piece of string?! Although they look cheap to register, patents can be expensive to maintain, running into hundreds of thousands of pounds if you want to take your concept worldwide. So they tend to suit ideas that have big market potential.

By contrast, registered designs might cost just a few hundred pounds. But they are a weaker form of protection – they can't block someone else from tweaking your design and taking the same basic concept to market. Registering your own trademark costs just a couple of hundred pounds.

The IPO website has a basic confidentiality agreement you can download for free and amend to suit your specific needs, to protect your ideas in discussions.

**TOP TIP!** *Learn about the different forms of IP right at the start – it'll stand you in good stead.*

**Q**. *At what stage in the business set-up should I seek protection?*

**A**. Right at the start you should learn about the different forms of IP and how protection works. The insights you gain could drastically affect how you shape your business and its future ability to be distinctive, block competitors, scale up, and command pricing that will earn you profits.

**Q**. *Would you recommend taking advice via the IPO website or commissioning an IP expert?*

**A**. Definitely learn the basics from the IPO website first, and also The British Library's Business and IP Centre in London. Make use of the free first sessions provided by IP experts to ask detailed questions. But always, always, before you commission an IP expert, absorb as much as you can from the experience of seasoned entrepreneurs and inventors. Understanding the subtleties of how IP protection actually works in business is essential if you want to grow a sustainable, thriving enterprise.

### Useful links

- ❀ She's Ingenious! | **www.shesingenious.org**
- ❀ Intellectual Property Office | **www.ipo.gov.uk**
- ❀ British Library Business & IP Centre | **www.bl.uk/bipc**

# HOUSEHOLD ADMIN

With a business plan prepared, the regulatory bodies informed and your intellectual property protected, it's time to take care of the household admin and make friends with the neighbours!

Over 60% of businesses are started from home on account of the low costs and lack of commute. When you start and grow your business from home, you may have a few questions about whom you need to inform. Here are the answers.

**Q**. *Do I need planning permission?*

**A**. You'll need planning permission to base the business at home if you answer 'yes' to any of these questions:

- ❀ will your home no longer be used mainly as a private residence?
- ❀ will your business result in a marked rise in traffic or people calling?
- ❀ will your business involve any activities that are unusual in a residential area?
- ❀ will your business disturb the neighbours at unreasonable hours or create other forms of nuisance such as noise or smells?

If your house is pretty much going to remain a house, with your business quietly accommodated within it, then permission shouldn't be required. If you're unsure, contact your local council to seek their views.

❀ Planning Portal | **www.planningportal.gov.uk**

**Q.** *Do I need to tell the local authority I'm working from home?*

**A.** This depends on whether you pass the planning test. If you need planning permission, you'll have to inform your local authority. If you don't, then the only benefit of telling them is that they'll charge you business rates (rather than council tax) on the part of the house being used for business purposes. Business rates are different in each area and something that should be discussed with your local authority.

❀ Business rates information from Business Link | **www.businesslink.gov.uk/businessrates**

**Q.** *Do I need to tell the landlord?*

**A.** Yes, it's best to let them know that you will be working from home. The good news is that the coalition government announced on 1 November 2010 that social landlords should review any contracts prohibiting people from running a business from home.

**Q.** *Do I need to inform my mortgage provider?*

**A.** Yes, it's best to let them know – even though it shouldn't mean any change in the mortgage repayment.

**Q.** *What about my insurance provider? Do they need to know?*

**A.** Yes, do inform your insurance company. Tell them about the equipment and stock you have at home. An upgrade from a domestic to a business policy is not usually expensive so don't be put off in making this call. Your insurance provider is likely to recommend that you also take out public liability insurance in case anyone who comes to visit suffers an injury in or around your home office. See page 65 for details of the type of insurance you may need.

**Q.** *Do I need protection for when customers and contacts come to visit?*

**A.** Yes, carry out a health and safety check, which is easy to do by following the steps set out by the Health and Safety Executive in their homeworking guide (PDF available at **www.hse.gov.uk/pubns/indg226.pdf**).

❀ Health and Safety Executive | **www.hse.gov.uk**

**Q.** *Should I tell the neighbours?*

**A.** Yes. See the next section for more advice!

## EVERYONE NEEDS GOOD NEIGHBOURS

When working from home it's worth keeping your neighbours sweet and firmly on side. You don't want them getting annoyed by any deliveries or unusual distractions.

Explain to your neighbours that you are running a business from home and that it shouldn't cause them any disturbance. (If it will cause them disturbance, see above: you'll need planning permission!)

Keep your promise and try to keep disruptions to a minimum. Avoid big heavy deliveries at anti-social hours and streams of client traffic clogging up the roads.

If the business reaches a major milestone, maybe host a party for your neighbours. A friend of mine said his neighbours were more than happy to 'be on the telly' when his home business appeared on a Sky News live broadcast from his home office!

Make friends with other homeworkers in your neighbourhood, so you can demonstrate together that the way you work is beneficial to the economy of the area and its safety, for example you can keep an eye on your neighbours' houses during the day.

If you know of a time when there will be an unusual amount of activity in your home office, let your neighbours know in advance and perhaps send a bottle of wine to thank them for their cooperation.

## TIP: THE BENEFITS OF A HOME-BASED BUSINESS

*There are benefits to the business, and to your life, in starting a business from home:*

### Work benefits

*The 60-second commute!*

*Getting more done, without distractions*

*The financial savings*

*Being able to give your clients personal service and a homely welcome when they visit the office*

*Adding to the property value of your home (research carried out on my website showed that homes with offices sell for an average £25,000 more than homes without offices)*

### Life benefits

*Feeling happier, healthier and more balanced, and enjoying the benefits this brings to your relationships*

*Wearing what you like*

*Dancing in the office!*

*Being a friend to the environment*

*Going shopping when there are no queues*

# CHAPTER FOUR
## TECH AND HOME
## OFFICE SET-UP

# SETTING UP WITH IT

**B**UILDING the right IT system for your business needn't mean starting from scratch or spending lots of money. Once your business grows you can upgrade your technology as and when funds become available. To start with, there are affordable, even free, solutions that can get you up and running in no time at all.

Chances are that you have some of them already!

## HARDWARE

Hardware is the physical components of your IT system. At a basic level, it includes things like your keyboard and mouse, but can extend to include printers, speakers, a VOIP phone, etc., but the basic component of a start-up IT system is your computer!

When starting out, using your home's shared computer will be just fine. Bear in mind, however, that in the first few months of starting your business you may find yourself working more hours than usual, trying to get it all set up – so prepare friends and family you live with for the possibility of reduced access!

Also, when your business grows, the data you accumulate – information on your customers, clients and contacts, including financial details – will become more and more valuable. You might then think twice about sharing your computer with the rest of the family.

For that reason, and for increased flexibility in when and where you can work, I'd recommend looking into buying a separate laptop computer if you don't have one already. There was a time when doing so was much more expensive than buying a desktop computer, but in recent years the prices have almost levelled off. Budget laptops start at around £300, but when buying computers it's usually beneficial to buy the best that you can afford. Buying the best will help you prepare for the future when new software is released with new demands on your hardware; it'll help you run more programs at once, and hold more data as your business grows; and it'll take the sting out of your purchase when prices start to drop in a few months time!

## ON THE MOVE

With the right technology for your office, it's time to take it outside! If you ever get tired of your four walls, it's good to know it's possible to work elsewhere. With a few simple tips and tricks you can enjoy unprecedented flexibility, and work almost anywhere: from your local coffee shop to the public park.

Here's how to keep your enterprise on the go away from the office.

If you already have a fairly up-to-date laptop computer, you have much of what you really need to work on the move. Most can pick up wireless internet access from receivers already built-in. If you have a slightly older laptop you can buy a small adaptor which you plug into a spare USB port.

Affordable options are available from a company called Belkin, who provide pretty clear instructions to help you get started.

❀ Belkin | **www.belkin.com/uk**

The other thing to consider investing in is a spare battery. Take a fully charged laptop on the go, and a fully charged spare battery, and you'll be able to keep working away from your desk all day. Some modern laptops (particular netbooks) have such a long battery life that this might not be necessary, but it's good to have as a back up.

## ACCESSING WI-FI HOTSPOTS

Nowadays, if you use your laptop computer in a public place like a coffee shop, a library, or even some public parks, you'll find that you can connect to a Wi-Fi hotspot. These are wireless internet connections that allow you to surf the web, check your email and instant message when you're away from your home office.

Unless you've a kindly local council who provide Wi-Fi hotspots free of charge, the chances are the hotspots you'll come across will cost you something. They usually charge for one hour's access, for 24 hours, or for a month at a time, and prices do vary.

## EVERYTHING FROM ANYWHERE

If you already use web mail, you'll be accustomed to the idea of your messages and contacts being available from any computer connected to the internet. So, how about running your entire business from any computer anywhere?

Web applications are programs that run online rather than on your computer. You run them through your web browser and all the data is stored on the internet so, in effect, you can access them and your information from pretty much any computer anywhere! The best example is provided by Google, whose Google Apps offering includes email, instant messaging, a calendar, word processor, spreadsheet and presentation software, as well as a website builder.

All the work you do is stored online so you can log in and out from anywhere and see the same information. Also, if your computer crashes or you buy a new system you won't lose any data or have to reinstall it on a new machine.

Google Apps is free to use and easy to set up.

❀  Google Apps for Business | **www.google.com/a**

**10 FREE CLOUD APPS FOR YOUR BUSINESS**

Cloud apps are not only fantastically useful, they generally don't take up room on your computer and you don't have to worry about backing up your data. They're also, more often than not, free to use.

Here are ten of our favourite free cloud apps for business.

**1** **Dropbox (www.dropbox.com)** Dropbox is like a thumb drive in the sky. It's a folder that sits on your computer but its contents are also stored remotely and synced across other computers and devices that are signed into your Dropbox account. No-nonsense sharing if you're working with others, and peace of mind that your work is backed up.

**2** **Evernote (www.evernote.com)** Evernote is a bit like Dropbox but for your brain. It helps you "remember everything" by allowing you to capture notes and ideas, photos and screen grabs, sounds and links, sync them automatically to the cloud and access them from practically anywhere – great for the planning stages of your business.

**3** **Google Docs (docs.google.com)** As broadband gets quicker and more reliable, Google Docs is becoming a bit of a threat to Microsoft Office: it includes apps for word processing, spreadsheets, presentations, drawings and forms – except all the apps run inside your browser, rather than on your desktop. All of your work is stored in the cloud and it's super easy to collaborate with others in real time on the same document.

**4** **Gmail (mail.google.com) and Google Calendar (calendar.google.com)** Gmail is Google's excellent online mail system, similar to Hotmail and Yahoo! etc., but did you know Google also make excellent calendar software? Both are really useful if you plan to work on the move.

**5** **Google Analytics (www.google.com/analytics)** When your website is up and running you'll want to know how many people are visiting. Google Analytics, like most of Google's services, is free, and helps you understand your website statistics, including where your visitors are from, which pages they visited the most, and how they found your website in the first place.

**6** **HootSuite (www.hootsuite.com)** If social media is part of your marketing plan – and it probably is! – there's no better way to manage your social media presence than with HootSuite. It keeps you on top of your Twitter, Facebook and LinkedIn accounts, as well as what your customers and potential customers are saying about your business.

**7** **Delicious (www.delicious.com)** Delicious is a bookmarking service that keeps all your important links in the cloud.

**8** **Toodledo (www.toodledo.com)** There's so much to do when starting a business but you can keep on top of all your tasks with this app. Get tasks out of your inbox by forwarding them to your Toodledo email address, organise them by folders, tags, context and subtasks, and sync them with your smartphone.

**9** **Basecamp (www.basecamp.com)**  If some tasks involve other people and form part of larger projects, check out this project management software. It allows you to share files, deliver projects on time and keep communication organised and out of your inbox.

**10** **MailChimp (www.mailchimp.com)**  To make sure your business message is in other people's inbox, put together a newsletter with MailChimp, send it out to your customer mailing list and track its success. Just make sure people have signed up to your mailing list before hitting 'send'!

# CREATING THE PERFECT WORK ENVIRONMENT

Wherever you've chosen to set up shop, create the perfect work environment by following this quick checklist to ensure you're working profitably and productively.

## FIND DEDICATED SPACE

Try to create an area at home that functions as your dedicated workspace. That way you can better adjust into business mode. It's also useful for making clear to friends and family that when you're in your home office, you're working. This dedicated space could be a spare room, in the attic, under the stairs, or even the garden shed. For garden office dwellers, one blog you might like is Shedworking (**www.shedworking.co.uk**).

## INVEST IN A GOOD DESK AND CHAIR

You could be spending a good few hours each day in your chair at your desk, so ensure they're both sturdy and comfortable. Buy a chair that's designed for computer use – and try it out first.

Back experts say your feet should be flat on the floor and your back straight. When it comes to computers, the top of your monitor or laptop screen should be at eye level and about an arm's length away from you. There are all sorts of docks and the like that can help with this, but there's also no harm in using a sturdy pile of books and an external mouse/keyboard to achieve the same end.

## HAVE A VISION

Put a vision board up on the wall and stick pictures on it that represent your personal and business ambitions: places you want to visit, targets for the company, and people you enjoy spending time with. Glance at it each day to remind yourself of everything you're working for.

### TIP: GET GREEN (AND FURRY)!

*Having plants in your home office can reduce work stress, experts say. Seeing a growth in greenery can also help you feel less alone, and it helps with humidity levels, dust and productivity. Likewise, pets are known to reduce stress and can be an excellent source of company!*

# LEAVING HOME

If an external office is right for you from the start then visit **www.startupbritain.org/spaces** to find available space in enterprise hubs, coworking spaces, government buildings and serviced offices. All needs and budgets catered for!

# CHAPTER FIVE
## STARTING ON A
## BUDGET
## AND BASIC FINANCIAL
## PLANNING

# STARTING ON A BUDGET

Y ou probably already have much of what you need to get started – i.e. a computer, mobile phone, some craft tools – so you may not need to buy much more equipment, depending on your business. Here are some tips for keeping initial costs low.

## START THE BUSINESS FROM HOME

Why take on the cost of an office when your spare room/attic/garden shed will do just as well? Think of the money you'll save: no premises, no commute, no overpriced sandwiches at lunchtime…! We've already talked about the admin side of starting from home and how to turn a home office into the perfect working environment. Plus if you have children, you can work the business around them so that you get the most out of your time together – not to mention the savings on childcare!

Sarah Cuthbertson was influenced by her mum in starting Just Brownies and has found running a business and taking care of her daughter can go hand-in-hand . . .

# MONEY MAKER

**NAME**: Sarah Cuthbertson

**TALENT**: Baking

**BUSINESS**: Just Brownies

SARAH CUTHBERTSON was a chef for over 14 years and always enjoyed making desserts. After coming across a brownie recipe with fresh chilli in it, she tweaked it and began making batches for family and friends for birthday and Christmas gifts.

> "Every time I gave my mum a batch she told me, 'You really should do this as a business'. But I had no idea how to start a business, and quite frankly I was scared to, being a single parent working full time to support my daughter."

However, a couple of months later Sarah decided to walk away from her job and one night she sat and designed a website and sent it to her Mum.

> "The next day there was a knock at the door, and there was my Mum with a cheque for £100. She told me to go out and buy some chocolate and extra baking trays."

Just Brownies took off from there! Sarah used Facebook to create a stir in her local village and among family and friends, and decided to organise a launch night for her new business held in memory of Ruth, a friend who had recently passed away. Sarah invited everyone she knew, including Ruth's family and people from St Barnabas, the local hospice. She also invited local newspapers to cover the event.

> "We had regular brownies for sale and also a heart-shaped version which people could have for a donation to the charity."

From there Just Brownies grew, but Sarah wanted to expand the business even further!

"I knew I couldn't sustain a business on friends and family orders alone so I started approaching local farmers' markets but the cake stall market was saturated, so I, being stubborn, stamped my foot and started my own very small local produce fayre in my village which gave me, as well as other small businesses in the area, an outlet to sell products from."

Sarah also tried the approach of taking her produce into a local supermarket and inviting them to stock it.

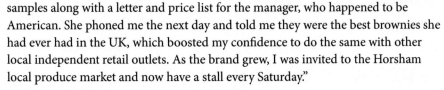

"I took the brave approach of walking into my closest supermarket and left a bag of samples along with a letter and price list for the manager, who happened to be American. She phoned me the next day and told me they were the best brownies she had ever had in the UK, which boosted my confidence to do the same with other local independent retail outlets. As the brand grew, I was invited to the Horsham local produce market and now have a stall every Saturday."

In addition to the local fairs and markets, Just Brownies has a strong presence with the local media.

"I've had fantastic coverage and support from the village magazine and Horsham's local newspaper, who have followed my progress from the start. They both now use me as a local business to support them with prizes, for example trick-or-treat themed brownies at Halloween."

Although Sarah has tried adverts in the local press and magazines, she thinks it is the editorial coverage that has more impact, as people like to read a story which sticks in their minds.

Sarah has also come up with a loyalty card scheme where customers can collect 'Brownie Points' for a free brownie after ten purchases. This, plus getting to know her customers, is what Sarah thinks really works for her business.

> "I try getting to know my customers by engaging in conversation with them and making them feel special. I also pop in the odd free brownie if it's their birthday, or to cheer them up if they are sad."

Based on this kind of customer service, it looks likely Sarah's customers will remain loyal!

**TOP TIP!** *"Do lots of research, talk to people and don't be afraid!"*

❀ **www.justbrownies.co.uk**

❀ **www.facebook.com/justbrownies**

❀ **@justbrownies**

# EMBRACE SOCIAL MEDIA

Make the most of free or low-cost technology tools to raise your profile and make sales. Twitter, Facebook and LinkedIn are excellent places to shout about your work, display photographs and interact with customers and other crafters. Page 147 onwards offers details of the major social media tools and how they can best be used to your benefit.

# BEG, BORROW AND BARTER!

When starting out, access all the resources you can. Need a space in which to host an event? Approach someone who has the space and would welcome the footfall you can bring. After some heavy duty equipment that your start-up budget just can't afford? Reach out to someone who has the equipment and ask whether you can use it in their downtime hours. It is perfectly possible to put together a business/event/project through bartering your way to success!

# WORK 5 TO 9

You can plan the business, register the business and indeed continue to run the business successfully by 'working 5 to 9' – this is the term I apply to the five-million-plus people who are holding down a day job and building a business at night and during weekends. While you might work as an estate agent during the day, you could get your pottery business up and running in your spare time, giving you the financial security of your full-time job and allowing you to build the new business at your own pace.

Working 5 to 9 is a very sensible way to start and grow – you give yourself the time to build confidence and cash flow in the business, plus you can keep putting money aside until you're ready to go full time.

If you are keeping hold of the day job and growing the business in your spare time, here's what you need to do regarding your current job and boss.

## The contract

If you have written terms and conditions of employment they are likely to contain reference to the pursuit of personal business ventures outside your contracted working hours. The clauses to look out for include 'the employee's duties and obligations' and what is commonly known as 'whole time and effort'. These clauses usually require the employee to devote the whole of their time, attention and abilities to the business of the employer.

If your contract contains these or similar clauses, don't despair, as it doesn't necessarily mean you can't pursue your business. Many employment contracts are drafted using standard templates with little consideration to personal circumstance.

 Don't despair if your work contract has scary clauses. Most are there because it's from a template. They can be negotiated."

You know your job better than anyone, so if you don't think your business venture will affect the way you do your job, it probably won't – and your employer will recognise this.

Having checked how things stand in the contract, it's time to talk things through with your boss.

## The conversation

Treat it as an amicable and informal conversation to gauge your employer's initial reaction.

I asked Patrick Lockton, a qualified lawyer, for his take on the matter and advice on how employees should go about having this conversation:

"When you approach your employer, be prepared to negotiate, be flexible and compromise. If you think it appropriate, make it clear your business venture will in no shape or form affect your ability to do your job or affect your employer's interests. If anything, it will make you a better, more confident and experienced employee and it will not cost your employer a thing."

Patrick goes on to say:

"After having such a conversation, you can do one of two things:

**1.** If your employer has not expressed any concerns about your intentions and you have no concerns of your own, disclose your intentions to your employer anyway. Treat it as something you want to do for the sake of clarity and for the record, as opposed to something you want their permission for.

**2.** If your employer has expressed concerns, try and negotiate a package that you are both happy with. Address their concerns, agree some ground rules and get their permission in writing. Give your employer as much helpful information as possible. If you are going to need some time off or to change your hours then this is the time to bring it up.

Always take written notes so that you don't forget what was said and so you can remind your employer what was agreed."

So long as you're not competing with your employer or breaching their trust, you shouldn't have any problem at all in pursuing your 5 to 9 ambitions. After all, as Patrick says, your employer benefits from all the new skills you're picking up, and it doesn't cost them a penny in training or resources!

Emma Maudsley started Sock Monkey Emporium whilst holding down a day job and has built the business to the point where she's working on it full time . . .

# MONEY MAKER

**NAME**: Emma Maudsley

**TALENT**: Handmade crafts

**BUSINESS**: Sock Monkey Emporium

Established in 2010, EMMA MAUDSLEY'S Sock Monkey Emporium has grown at pace, with monkeys travelling to the USA, Canada, Australia, New Zealand and Singapore!

However, Emma's business story began after she needed to raise some cash to buy a second-hand car after passing her driving test. "I had seen a few other people making sock monkeys on Facebook and thought I would give it a go," Emma recalls. Her first order came in and she hasn't looked back since.

> "People kept ordering them so I kept making them! I gave up my full-time job a year later!"

Finding her first customer through Facebook set the tone for the business as Emma finds most of her orders come through the social networking site, allowing Emma to sell all around the world – "Facebook is perfect for gaining worldwide exposure" – and with over 4,500 likes, Emma has an engaged community keen to see the latest designs and hear her news. Emma also has an Etsy shop and is a member of The Artisan Group, a company based in LA, which is a juried group of talented artisans from around the world who participate in gift lounges prior to events such as The Oscars and The Golden Globes. Through membership of this group Emma has been able to send her products to celebrities such as Beyoncé, Jessica Alba, Uma Thurman and Denise Richards amongst others.

A key part to the success of Sock Monkey Emporium is the quality of the products she makes and the customer service on offer: "Repeat customers are very important and supplying a quality product along with good customer service is key." Emma works alone and every monkey is handmade, meaning this business owner has to plan her time effectively to be able to supply orders and make as many monkeys as possible.

"I have had to withdraw from supplying shops as demand for monkeys is so high. I have adapted my selling policy so I am able to make as much stock as possible during the week to take with me to craft fairs and then sell the remaining stock on Facebook the same evening. Custom orders are carried out from September 1st to allow people to get monkeys for Christmas gifts."

Emma has ambitious plans for Sock Monkey Emporium:

"I would like to make more business mascots as it allows me to explore my creativity. I have also started making handbags from upcycled men's ties and would like to be able to make more of these."

With so much in the pipeline, this busy monkey is staying safely out of trouble!

**TOP TIP!** *"Embrace social media. I have not had to pay for any marketing or promotional campaigns yet I am able to sell on a global platform!"*

❀ **www.facebook.com/SockMonkeyEmporium**

❀ **@SockMonkeyEmp**

# MANAGING YOUR MONEY

It's become so much easier to start a business on a budget and keep finances in check by keeping overheads low. This section shows you how to manage your funds, as well as offering a simple way to calculate profit through use of a basic spreadsheet.

## STRAIGHTFORWARD FINANCE

When planning a business you need to be sure earnings are higher than outgoings. Earnings are also referred to as revenue, turnover or income and this should be a greater figure than outgoings, overheads or costs. Let's look at the items that come within each category.

### Incoming

Earn by selling your product or service and any associated income opportunities. For example, you set up a business selling unique handmade cushions. From the outset, earn income from:

❀ Selling 24 x handmade cushions at £25 per cushion = £600 income per week

❀ Speaking at events to teach others how to make cushions = £150 per event

❀ Custom requests, e.g. a unique and one-off production = £75 per item

❀ Developing a blog on the topic of cushions that attracts cushion-istas as readers and paying advertisers as your secondary customers = £priceless!

### Outgoings

Here are the costs; some payable at start-up stage and others that are ongoing:

❀ Salary – how much do you need to pay yourself? (You may be pleasantly surprised at how thriftily you can live when not commuting.)

❀ Property – start the business from home and avoid the cost of a pricey second office.

❀ Raw materials and equipment – what are the materials you need to deliver and promote your finished cushions? And do you need any equipment to make that product; a sewing machine, computer, printer, smartphone or camera?

❀ Insurance – be insured from the start and choose a policy that covers all your needs.

❀ Website/promotion materials – we will cover on page 53 onwards (chapters five, six and seven) how you can build a home on the web and promote the business on a shoestring of a budget.

## BE INSURED

There are different categories of insurance which you need to know about to secure the policy that's right for you. The main ones are:

❀ **Professional indemnity** – Relevant to businesses offering services and knowledge and provides protection if you receive a claim alleging a negligent act, error or omission committed by you in the course of the conduct of your professional business.

❀ **Public liability** – Advisable to have if clients are visiting your home office and/or you are supplying goods to consumers. This will protect you in the event of potential injury to business visitors and/or damages arising from the supply or sale of goods which have caused injury to a third party or their property.

❀ **Business interruption** – Covers your potential loss of revenue following a material damage loss.

❀ **Employer's liability** – Only applies when you have employees and offers protection in the event of death or injury to them sustained in the course of their employment.

❀ **Motor** – This is different to standard car insurance, which does not include business use. If you have a vehicle dedicated to carrying stock and/or products, you should buy motor insurance or get a business extension on your car insurance policy when using your existing car for business travel.

❀ **Home** – You probably already have home insurance but this will generally not cover business activities carried out at home or business equipment within the home. Speak to your insurance provider and upgrade to a business policy. This is not usually costly but it will ensure you're protected.

## MANAGING CASH FLOW

Managing cash flow is crucial for the survival of the business, so in order to stay on top of this, keep records of all incomings and outgoings in a basic spreadsheet.

Here is an example spreadsheet you can adapt:

| Date | Client | Work | Amount (incl. VAT?) | Invoice no. | Date sent | Date settled |
|------|--------|------|---------------------|-------------|-----------|--------------|
|      |        |      |                     |             |           |              |
|      |        |      |                     |             |           |              |
|      |        |      |                     |             |           |              |

Keeping records up to date and being on top of invoices means you'll have positive cash flow and be in a position to buy the stock and supplies needed to make the business function.

The most common reasons for a disruption to cash flow are customers that don't pay, not selling enough products or having too many outgoings, so what can you do to avoid this?

---

### TIP: HOW TO STAY ON TOP OF YOUR CASH FLOW

❀ *Try to do your cash flow budget regularly so that you always have a clear idea about where your business stands.*

❀ *Save costs where possible – you will need to spend some money to get the business up and running but try to keep these to a minimum so outgoings don't start to rack up.*

❀ *Have customers pay before you ship their items.*

❀ *Plan effectively – if you know there is a craft fair coming up that you want to attend but it might eat into your budget, start planning for this a couple of months early so when the time comes, it isn't a big outgoing expense.*

---

See page 19 for a template invoice and how to keep a record of invoices raised and amounts paid.

# PRICING PRODUCTS

When pricing items you don't want to be pricing too high and putting off customers nor do you want to price too low so you don't make any money! There isn't one simple solution and many people will approach this differently, but what's key is to account for the time you take to produce each item; factor this in and price competitively against what others are charging in the market.

Let's take the example of making a handbag and look at how you would work up a price:

The cost for **materials** including fabric, thread, company labels, zips/buttons and embellishments comes to £3. When deciding how much your materials cost, you don't need to take into account the total price of the supply if you only used a fraction of it. For example, you were able to buy the fabric for the handbags at £2 per metre, but you've only used 1/2 a metre per bag. The cost for the fabric per handbag should therefore be £1.

You then need to add the cost of your **time**. Say it takes one hour for you to make each handbag and you think that your hourly rate is roughly £7.

Now that you have your £10 base cost for your product (£3 for all the materials plus £7 for labour), you need to decide how much you want to **mark it up** in order to sell to customers.

Many crafters use the 2.5 formula, whereby you multiply base cost by 2.5 and use that as your price. In our example this would make the handbag £25. Once you have that figure, you need to look at your competitors in more detail – are they offering anything similar, and are their products of a similar quality, size and style? Depending on the results of this research, you may want to revise your price, either increasing it if you think your product is worth more, or decreasing it to make it more competitive.

> Many crafters use the 2.5 formula to price their products."

Over time, you may decide you have developed your skill and are producing superior items or sourcing more unique materials so would like to increase prices. Don't be afraid to do this as people will recognise they are buying a unique handmade product and be willing to pay a little extra.

# SOURCING SUPPLIES AND EQUIPMENT

As with most aspects of the business, research is key! Search online for cost-effective and reliable suppliers and by asking around for personal recommendations.

For example, if you want to run a cake business, you could search online for cake supplies and find companies such as:

❀ Cakes, Cookies & Crafts | **www.cakescookiesandcraftsshop.co.uk**

❀ Cake Craft World | **www.cakecraftworld.co.uk**

❀ Cake Craft Shop | **www.cakecraftshop.co.uk**

Or if you want to make invitations, you can find stationery suppliers, such as:

❀ The Handcraft Card Company | **www.thehandcraftedcardcompany.co.uk**

❀ Kooky Kards | **www.kookykards.com**

❀ Paper Crafter | **www.papercrafter.co.uk**

These are just a selection of what can be found from a quick online search.

Online sales sites can also be a great place to source materials. Check out the following:

❀ Etsy | **www.etsy.com**

❀ eBay | **www.ebay.co.uk**

❀ Alibaba | **www.alibaba.co.uk**

When looking at sourcing supplies, think about how much you're actually going to use. Even though it's generally more cost-effective, you don't want to interrupt cash flow by buying too much in terms of material and then not receiving the money in from sales, especially if your product has a longer lead time. Alternatively, if buying in smaller quantities, be confident you can get extra supplies quickly if necessary so customers aren't kept waiting!

When it comes to sourcing equipment, if you can't afford to buy new machinery or tools, don't rule out buying second-hand – auction sites, car boot sales and recycling websites are useful places to look. Talk to other business owners as they may be up for sharing tools or upgrading to new equipment and looking for an opportunity to pass on their tools, meaning you get sound equipment at a reduced price.

# 10 FINANCE TIPS FOR CRAFT AND HANDMADE BUSINESSES

EMILY COLTMAN ACA, Chief Accountant to super-straightforward online accounting system FreeAgent and author of *Finance for Small Business*, offers her top ten financial tips for craft-based businesses . . .

> As a craft business you'll almost certainly be buying and selling stock. This might be raw materials; for example, if you're making curtains, then your raw materials would be the lining fabric, curtain fabric, thread and trimmings. Or you might buy in stock to sell on as is, for example if you're importing silk kaftans from Thailand.

## 1. Choose your accounting system wisely

It's important for any business to keep their books in order from day one, but for owners of craft businesses this is even more important than usual as you'll be dealing with stock and you'll need to keep track of how much you have at any one time.

Choose a good accounting system with the right level of stock control for your business.

If you're buying in stock to sell straight on, you'll need a system with light stock control. In which case, try FreeAgent (**www.freeagent.com**).

If you're making products from raw materials, particularly if your business is growing, look for a system with in-depth stock control. I like Brightpearl (**www.brightpearl.com**) for this.

## 2. Be careful with commission sales

You may sell your products to larger organisations such as countywide craft bodies, who will then sell on the items to the public. If you're going to do this, make sure the rate of commission they keep on the sales is fair, and that the interim buyer pays you on time. Don't be caught out by big companies who may pay "low and slow".

## 3. Beware of VAT registration if you sell to the public

If you're selling your goods directly to the public, for example via your own website, don't register for VAT unless and until you have to (see **www.hmrc.gov.uk/vat**) because to the public VAT just represents an increase on the cost of your product.

## 4. Save money where you can

If your business won't take up much space, start from home and find out whether you can save money by buying large items for your business second-hand. For example, if you want to make pottery, could you find a potter's wheel for sale on eBay or Gumtree, or even pay to use the wheel at your local art college, rather than buy a new one? But choose your cost savings wisely – see point 5.

## 5. Choose suppliers carefully

When you're thinking of how much you should pay for stock, don't just look for the cheapest option. Think also of quality and ease of acquisition. For example, it may be cheaper to buy your buttons for your homemade childrenswear from abroad, but if they break when tugged by a child, that's bad news for your brand and you could lose business. And there could be myriad reasons (stray ash clouds, political upheavals) why your imported stock can't reach you. There may be import tax too, which would push up the total price paid, so choose your suppliers carefully.

## 6. Think about how much stock you should buy in at a time

Suppliers may well give a discount if you buy a larger quantity, and you'll save on postage too, but make sure you don't end up with a pile of unsellable stock which will put a dent in your profit and tie up cash. Your stock might not be perishable, but if you're making fabric bags and you buy a large quantity of bright orange material, will bright orange stay in fashion long enough for you to make the bags and sell them?

## 7. Work out your profitable lines

If you sell more than one kind of product, for example hand-knitted mittens and scarves, it's a good idea to know which lines bring in the most profit, as that's where you should look to focus your time. To work out how profitable each line is, take your sale price per unit (for example, £10 per scarf), then subtract how much each unit costs to make.

Make sure you include all your costs. For example, if you're making patchwork cushions, think of not only the fabric and thread but also the cushion pad and zip, and don't forget to include your time for cutting out and sewing up. The more intricate the design, the longer this will take.

Use a spreadsheet to help you and ideally do this before you set your prices to customers, because it can be very hard to put prices up right away.

## 8. Set your prices carefully for handmade goods

How much premium can you charge for handmade goods? For example, if you are making bespoke cross-stitch wedding samplers then your customers will expect these to be sewn by hand, and will expect to pay a premium because this will take you a long time. But if you're making clothes then these would usually be machine-stitched, which would not take as long to make as handsewn garments.

## 9. Your website or mine?

Should you sell through your own website or through sites such as Etsy or Alibaba? In terms of costs, weigh up the price of building your own site (possibly by using a dedicated e-commerce platform such as those outlined from page 106) or having it built by a professional, against the greater pool of customers you'll find through Etsy but will pay fees for. And don't forget that if you go through your own website you'll also have to invest time marketing the site and maintaining it, or paying someone to do that for you.

## 10. Plan for the future

No matter how small your business is, it's very important to plan and forecast your sales, costs, profit, and cash coming in and out. This isn't just for large businesses. You won't be able to keep everything in your head no matter how small your business is so write it down and record it!

# MONEY MAKER

**NAME**: Joanna Michaelides

**HOBBY**: Baking

**BUSINESS**: Just Puddings

JOANNA MICHAELIDES' business, Just Puddings, sprang out of her love of baking for her own children. She used her children's birthdays as an excuse to be creative. "So many people commented on the cakes that I thought it might be worth trying to sell them," she recalls, and the first person who bought was a parent from her son's school.

Working for herself was the perfect solution as it allowed Joanna the flexibility to work around her children's school day and activities whilst earning some extra money. "Working from home is a really convenient solution which allows me to multi-task whilst working." However, when Joanna is baking the kitchen is off-limits, which can be quite tricky with young children!

Joanna has big plans for the next couple of years.

> "I started my business slowly and it has grown organically purely through word-of-mouth. I am now confident in my product and ability and feel I am at a stage where I can expand whilst maintaining my personal touch. I plan to expand my client base through targeted marketing campaigns, advertising and references. I would also really like to cater for more corporate events and private parties. I am also planning to expand

my repertoire to include teaching classes. All this whilst retaining my business ethos – fresh, flavoursome and family!"

**TOP TIP!** *"Believe in yourself and your idea!"*

❀ **www.justpuddings.co.uk**

❀ **www.facebook.com/JustPuddings**

❀ **@JustPuddings**

# FUNDING

Following the budgeting steps in this chapter will certainly help your finances, but if you think you'll need funding all the same, there are a few places you can look.

## FRIENDS AND FAMILY

Friends and family are people you can trust – and asking them for money hopefully won't come with strings attached! Do consider having a written agreement, though, that covers the amount borrowed and a payback schedule.

## BANKS

Approach a bank and ask to speak to a small business advisor at your local branch. Take a copy of your business plan with you and be prepared to talk through it – remember, be clear about what your business does and explain how you can make money from it. It may help to run through this with a friend or colleague beforehand so that you feel prepared.

## STARTUP LOANS

If you're aged between 18 and 24, you'll like the sound of StartUp Loans which were launched by the government to lend funding to any young person wanting to start a business. Visit the StartUp Britain or StartUp Loans website for details on where and how to apply.

✿ StartUp Britain | **www.startupbritain.org**

✿ StartUp Loans | **www.startuploans.co.uk**

# CREDIT CARDS

Many a business has been started with help from a flexible friend, but you must shop for the best rates. It's a competitive market and the credit card companies are keen for your business. Make sure you are on time with repayments (to avoid penalty interest charges) and aim to pay back the credit as soon as you can and as sales start coming in. This route is suggested based on start-up costs being small and the ability to pay back at speed so avoiding monthly repayments at high interest rates.

## TIP: A CLEAR DIVISION

*It is a good idea to open a business bank account early on so you don't mix up your business and personal finances, which may complicate record keeping. To open a bank account you'll need to provide details of your business, a business plan and a certificate of incorporation for limited companies. Find out more about bank account opening requirements on the Business Link website:* **bit.ly/hh3war**

# GRANTS

There are grants available from a number of sources, including the government, European Union, local authorities, credit finance institutions and some charitable organisations, such as the Prince's Trust.

Find out more about grants and other help that may be available to you at:

❀ Business Link Finance Finder |
**improve.businesslink.gov.uk/resources/business-finance-finder**

❀ National Enterprise Network (with links to your local enterprise agency) |
**www.nationalenterprisenetwork.org**

❀ The Prince's Trust (funds available to help young people start a business) | **www.princes-trust.org.uk**

❀ PRIME (offers a Zopa-PRIME Olderpreneur Loan) | **www.prime.org.uk**

❀ J4b Grants (grants, loans and venture capital) | **www.j4bgrants.co.uk**

❀ StartUp Britain | **www.startupbritain.org**

❀ StartUp Loans | **www.startuploans.co.uk**

# CROWD FUNDING

Crowd funding is a relatively recent development that involves sourcing funds from a group of others, with each lending a proportion of the total you wish to borrow. Check out Crowdcube (**www.crowdcube.com**) or Seedrs (**www.seedrs.com**) where you can secure a loan from people willing to lend.

---

If you're aged 16–30, based in the UK and have been running a business for less than 12 months, apply for the Shell LiveWIRE Awards and be in with a chance of winning one of four monthly awards of £1,000 to spend on your business. Not only do you receive the award, you get profile too!

❀ **www.shell-livewire.org/awards/grand-ideas-awards**

---

# CHAPTER SIX
# SELLING

**S**ELL, sell, sell! You have your idea. It's supported by research and a plan pointing you in the right direction. You've sorted out all the technology you need to get going. And with the company registered and admin/finances in shape, it's time to get into business by making some noise and getting sales!

In this section we'll look at how you achieve sales by selling offline and online, via platform sites and then via your own site.

Follow these five steps to making offline sales.

## 1. Make a list

Draw on your existing resources, grab your address book and pull out the friends, family, colleagues and acquaintances you think might be interested in your product. Add to the list with details of local people and businesses.

## 2. Pitch up

Write to the people on your list and announce your new business venture. Consider this an opportunity to make your pitch, but don't be too pushy. And remember to address each recipient personally. No one likes a group email!

## 3. Follow up

Follow up in a few days time, either with another email or, better still, a phone call. Take some soundings as to the success of your pitch and react accordingly. If the potential customer or client sounds keen, go for it and arrange a meeting.

## 4. Meet up

Arrange a time and place to meet that's convenient for your potential customer or client – don't forget to take samples of your work. Be professional but also likeable.

They're equally important characteristics when making a sale.

If the customer agrees the deal, bring the meeting to a fairly speedy end. Your job is done – for now. It's time to head home and deliver on the promise you made with your first customer.

## 5. Make some noise

Once you've made your first sale – shout about it! If your new customer or client agrees, include them in a press release or write about them on your website or blog, so other potential customers or clients can see that you're well and truly in business!

---

### TIP: SALES ARE FLYING HIGH

*Have promotional flyers made to take to events or deliver through doors. Increase your chances of turning flyers into firm sales by:*

- *having a design that is memorable, possibly quirky and, ideally, that your potential customers will want to keep on their desktop/in their purse/atop the kitchen shelf*

- *making the offer clear and confirming the benefits of buying*

- *including a call to action, i.e. a way in which the interested customer can contact you.*

---

# PROMOTIONAL FLYERS

Getting your message to as many people as possible is key. Flyers are a cheap and quick way to do this. Stationery stores can normally print about 1,000 A5 flyers in half an hour; it's a cost-effective way to get your brand in front of people.

Marion Paterson and her daughter Emily McIntyre place a firm focus on customer care and service in their business. It keeps customers coming back for more . . .

# MONEY MAKER

**NAME**: Marion Paterson and Emily McIntyre

**TALENT**: Handmade Crafts

**BUSINESS**: Ruby & Rose Jewellery

Ruby & Rose Jewellery is a Scottish business run by mother and daughter team, MARION PATERSON and EMILY MCINTYRE. It all started as a therapeutic hobby after Marion was diagnosed with Dystonia, a rare neurological condition, in 2006. She had to give up work and driving as her condition worsened.

A few years later, Marion needed something to make to take to a fundraiser and remembered doing some beading with her granddaughter the previous week. She went to a local hobby shop, bought materials and put some designs together. All her pieces sold and Marion got the bug! From there, she started attending evening classes, developing her skills via online tutorials and buying books and magazines. At first she made pieces for herself to wear but friends and family soon started to ask where she was buying her jewellery. Once they realised Marion was the designer and creator, she started getting asked to make pieces for them, or for gifts, and the business began to take shape as daughter Emily persuaded her to turn the hobby into something more.

> "At this stage we thought it would just be something that helped to cover her costs, rather than actually make money. I started by setting up a Facebook page for the business and actively promoted the page by asking friends and family to share the page link with their friends and family. It started to grow that way and this is where our first customers were found."

Emily's role is to look after promotion whilst Marion continues to make the jewellery, with each drawing on their own personal strengths and interests.

"Starting a business can be expensive so we made the most of the free stuff! We started with a Facebook page and a free website. I also created a blog and later set up a page on Twitter – all wonderful forms of communication which can get you right to the heart of your customer base. As the business started to grow we decided we needed a professional brand so had a logo and website designed and developed for us."

Every piece of jewellery is handmade and limited edition so quality and customer satisfaction are key priorities.

"We are a small company so our customers aren't just order numbers to us, we appreciate every one of them. With our social media pages we are able to interact with them personally and love to hear from them and keep in touch."

Customers come from as far afield as Australia, Canada and America, which Emily credits to the internet: "It has helped us sell worldwide – our website, Facebook and

Twitter has brought us closer to customers all over the world."

These ladies have exciting plans for the future and want to keep growing Ruby & Rose with the ultimate ambition being "to make it a household name".

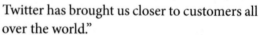

**TOP TIP #1!** *Emily: "Give your business a voice – people don't buy from a business they buy from a person, so show people who that person is, whether it's in a blog, on Twitter/Facebook or your packaging, website or stall front."*

**TOP TIP #2!** *Marion: "Don't give up. You will get knock downs but it's important to learn from them and move on. Don't dwell on them too much in case you lose focus."*

❀ **www.rubyandrosejewellery.com**

❀ **www.facebook.com/RubyandRoseJewellery**

❀ **@RRJewellery**

# SELLING INTO PHYSICAL STORES

Maybe you've started by selling products direct to customers at craft shows but what about making sales via local shops?

Before you approach any shops, make a list of appropriate places where you think your product could work well.

❀ Does your town have a gift shop or art gallery?

❀ Are there lots of boutiques that stock a range of different items?

❀ It's a good idea to think outside the box too: could your local coffee shop stock some of your items?

You won't have a 100% success rate in placing items, so prepare a longer list of targets than you think you'll need.

# 5 TOP TIPS FOR MARKET PLACEMENT

LAURA RIGNEY, founder of Pitcher House and Mumpreneur UK, and author of *Pitching Products for Small Business* (**www.enterprisenation.com/shop**) offers her five top tips for pitching your product effectively . . .

## 1. Be confident with pricing

Selling wholesale is a new ballpark as far as pricing is concerned. Make your product attractive to buyers with your pricing. A great way to show you're trying to help retailers is to set up a structured pricing system, i.e. 100 units or less £xx per unit, 101–500 units £yy per unit, and 501 units or more £zz per unit. This system could also encourage shops and buyers to place larger orders.

## 2. Understand your product inside out

This means technical data as well as knowing why someone would buy it. When you get a meeting with a buyer or approach a shop owner, talk with confidence about where the product is made, by who, and using what kind of materials. Remember there is pressure on large retailers to "go green", so the more you can offer that as a potential supplier the more attractive you will be.

## 3. Be prepared

If a buyer places an order, how quickly will you have manufacturing, distribution and storage in place? Buyers won't expect a new small business to have a giant factory sitting waiting for someone to press the "go" button but they will want a realistic estimate of how long it will be until your product is in their warehouses/on the shop shelf. Once you have given your timings, stick to them. Even if this means exaggerating the time it will take for them to be delivered. Better to be early rather than late!

## 4. Pitch perfect

If you're pitching in person, make it informative, exciting and interesting and where possible have samples, evidence of past sales and customer satisfaction. You need to know your figures without having to look through paperwork and be prepared to haggle a little on prices. If someone likes your product enough and you have sold it well enough they will buy it, even if it's a few pennies more than they would like to pay. In the other direction, sometimes it may be worth offering a larger than normal discount as a trial for their first order.

## 5. Stay listed

When a company takes on your product it's called being listed. Once you are listed the work is just beginning! It's now time to stay listed for as long as possible and the way to do this is through marketing and PR. The more you promote your product and the shops/galleries/boutiques that are selling them, the more they will be bought by consumers, thus encouraging buyers to place more orders with you!

---

**TIP: PITCHUP!**

*Apply to pitch to large retailers through the StartUp Britain PitchUp! Project where you can present your products direct to buyers and if not secure a contract, certainly secure feedback on your products and pitching technique!*

**www.startupbritain.org/highstreet**

---

Lucy Lee may not be selling in physical stores yet but she's selling online via platform sites and experimenting with flash sales and other online routes to market . . .

# MONEY MAKER

**NAME**: Lucy Lee

**TALENT**: Jewellery

**BUSINESS**: Lily Charmed

LUCY LEE's business Lily Charmed was born in August 2011 after Lucy decided she needed a life change. Having worked as a producer on BBC's *Strictly Come Dancing* and spent long hours away from home and family, Lucy decided she wanted to start a business that could work around her family life.

"I am not intimidated by starting new projects, and becoming an 'expert' on a subject through research – this is a skill that has seen me through many bizarre TV productions – but when I decided to start a business I knew it would be best to team up with a person with complementary skills and contacts, giving the business the best possible start.

My cousin Marcus was already running a successful jewellery business but had not ventured online as his items are often unique and not suited to the online retail environment. We teamed up and used his knowledge and contacts in jewellery design and manufacture with my bullishness and 'get it done' attitude to create a brand new business."

Lucy and Marcus wanted to create and develop a jewellery business that offered something new for customers.

"It needed to be something personal and meaningful, something that we would want to buy ourselves, and that would work online. Charm jewellery ticked all the boxes; it has timeless appeal, and with our unique presentation, and personalisation options, it really stood out from what was already on offer elsewhere."

The first customer came through NotOnTheHighStreet.com, a site through which Lily Charmed still sell their products: "It has worked fantastically well for us. NOTHS.com have a great marketing team and they've really helped us build a business".

Lucy has also developed Facebook and Twitter profiles for the business and uses affiliate marketing schemes to help drive traffic directly to the website. Tests are now being run with small ads in glossy magazines and inroads into the bridesmaid gift market via wedding magazines and websites.

"We hosted a Lily Charmed 'party', which was a great success, and we'll definitely organise more of these. We have also tried 'flash sales' via Achica.com and created bespoke message cards/necklace designs for boutique chain Mint Velvet, and *Red* Direct. If there were more hours in the day I would promote Lily Charmed even further!"

Lucy feels it's the emotional response to the jewellery that keeps customers coming back.

"When people are given a Lily Charmed piece as a gift, they are often so touched by the thought that has gone into choosing the charm and the personalised message that both the gift giver and receiver return to us. One lady bought a necklace for her sister, who teared up at the sentiment behind the gift, and then the next day she bought our entire range for her gift shop!"

As a result, Lily Charmed is selling internationally and Lucy is looking to expand into America in the next few years.

Although Lucy mostly works alone, when she needs help in the business she looks close to home.

> "I'm very lucky to have talented friends and family who have great skill sets such as photographic styling, bookkeeping, graphic design, marketing, etc. – so I use their skills when I can. Without the fabulousness and generosity of these people Lily Charmed would not exist."

Lucy is looking ahead to the future with optimism and confidence: "I would love to build on our current success with sales at trade shows, a busy Christmas, and basically finding new and interesting ways to introduce Lily Charmed to as many people as possible!"

**TOP TIP!** *"Cash flow is king! Make sure you keep a keen eye on money coming in and out, and plan accordingly. You can't grow your business without money in the bank!"*

❀   **www.lilycharmed.com**

❀   **www.facebook.com/pages/Lily-Charmed/199643666743066**

❀   **@LilyCharmedcom**

# SELLING ONLINE

Consider raising your profile and making sales via powerful platform sites before creating your own. There are a number of options and the upside is these sites attract customers on your behalf, and some of them attract customers from all over the world. Here are a number of websites that enable you to sell.

# EBAY

eBay has grown to become the largest shopping mall on the web. In 2012 there were 180,000 small businesses trading on the site in the UK, generating sales of £1.6 billion a year. The good thing is, having a store on eBay means you are opened up to an international audience and many potential customers!

**www.ebay.co.uk** | **@eBay**

# 5 TOP EBAY TIPS

Dan Wilson, eBay expert and author of *Make Serious Money on eBay UK*, offers five tips on how to make the most of the mega marketplace known as eBay:

### 1. Start small

Go slow until you've found your way. Start with a few, easy-to-post items and learn about eBay before boosting your range and prices. Don't stake too much on your first eBay bet.

### 2. Sell like you mean it

The eBay marketplace is competitive and you'll lose out unless you have top-notch listings. Craft fabulous item titles, upload impeccable pictures and write descriptions that tempt buyers. Be truthful and honest and look professional from the start.

### 3. Be quick off the mark

Buyers have come to expect great service. Dispatch orders quickly — preferably within 24 hours of payment — and well packed, and make sure you reply to emails and other communications swiftly, too. The quality and speed of your replies and dispatches has an impact on customer feedback.

### 4. Put a lid on postal costs

Understand postage and packaging costs and make sure you factor it in to your costs where necessary.

### 5. Loyalty means profit

When you're building your eBay business, encouraging repeat buyers is important. Once a buyer trusts you as an online seller, they're likely to keep coming back. Offer discounts and incentives with every dispatch and cross-market complementary products.

## ENTERPRISE NATION

The Enterprise Nation Directory connects you with customers and suppliers in the friendliest business community on the web. You can list your business in the directory for free. It's supported by a business blog, with tips and advice on sales and marketing, IT efficiency, productivity and motivation, and a community for all the help and support you need to start and grow your business.

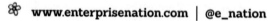 **www.enterprisenation.com | @e_nation**

## ALIBABA

Having a presence on this site enables you to buy and sell and source supplies with companies from across the globe. The site has visitors from 240 countries and regions, with over 1 million registered users in the UK. Through the site you can locate suppliers or make sales of your finished product direct to customers. Alibaba is a champion of international trade; carrying out research on the topic, providing a platform for traders to interact, and promoting overseas sales as a form of business that is wholly viable, regardless of company size.

**www.alibaba.com | @AlibabaTalk_UK**

## AMAZON MARKETPLACE

You may be used to buying from Amazon, but have you considered the site as a platform from which to sell? Have your products appear before millions of customers all around the world by signing up to Amazon Marketplace. It offers two sales options: a package for casual sellers who expect to sell less than 35 items a month (a fixed fee per sale plus a referral fee), and for more seasoned sellers there is the 'sell a lot' package, which has a monthly charge plus a referral fee for unlimited sales that do not have to be in the Amazon catalogue.

**www.amazon.co.uk/marketplace | @AmazonMarketPl**

## ISTOCKPHOTO

Want to sell your photography, illustrations, videos or music effects around the world? This is the site for you:

> "iStockphoto is the web's original source for royalty-free stock images, media and design elements. For over 10 years artists, designers and photographers from all over the world have come here to create, work and learn."

To start selling, all you have to do is join the site, apply to be a contributor and submit samples of your work. As a contributor, you receive a base royalty rate of 20% for each file downloaded, which goes up to 40% if you exclusively display work on the site.

**www.istockphoto.com**

# HANDMADE MARKETPLACES

A growing number of sites are dedicated to helping the artisan and handmade business owner sell goods across the globe.

- ❀ Etsy – "The world's handmade marketplace"
  **www.etsy.com | @Etsy**

- ❀ Not On The High Street – "One basket, hundreds of unique shops"
  **www.notonthehighstreet.com | @notonthehighst**

- ❀ Folksy – "Modern British Craft"
  **www.folksy.com | @Folksy**

- ❀ iCraft – "Creativity without borders"
  **www.icraft.ca | @iCraft**

- ❀ DaWanda – "Products with love"
  **en.dawanda.com | @DaWanda_en**

- ❀ ArtFire – "Premier handmade marketplace to buy & sell handmade crafts, supplies, vintage and art"
  **www.artfire.com | @Artfire**

- ❀ MISI – "Make It, Sell It"
  **www.misi.co.uk | @misi_uk**

- ❀ ShopHandmade – "Rewarding Creativity"
  **www.shophandmade.com | @shophandmade**

---

Increase the chances of having your products browsed and bought by uploading quality photos of your items.

---

Maggie Conway sells online via Etsy and her own site and is a true believer in the power of the web . . .

# MONEY MAKER

**NAME**: Maggie Conway

**TALENT**: Handmade Crafts/Jewellery

**BUSINESS**: Robin & Rose

MAGGIE CONWAY launched her candle and bath & body product business Robin and Rose in 2009, after realising the rising appreciation for all things handmade in the UK.

"Money is scarce and there is real support for 'Made in Britain' products rather than mass-produced items, with people willing to spend a little extra on a gift that is special and handcrafted."

Maggie's first sale was made at a great North London market called 'The Vintage Tea Party & Gift Fair' in Highgate, and since then Robin & Rose has supplied gifts and handmade crafts around the world.

"I have shipped orders to America, Australia and Europe through online stores and this is an area that I very much want to grow in the future."

Maggie currently sells her products at fairs and markets, through her own website, and online marketplace Etsy, which she thinks has contributed significantly to her success.

"Etsy in particular is a great platform as it drives traffic to my own site so it's up to the seller to offer and sell desirable products at the right price to attract the customer."

Maggie also promotes the business as much as she can, both online and off.

"I have found Twitter very helpful, otherwise nothing beats meeting customers face-to-face at markets – the personal touch of explaining and selling your product to the end user is priceless. Plus you see first-hand the reaction to new products and get feedback on what people are looking for so you can react quickly."

Although Maggie runs the business by herself and works alone, she has found the support of local designers and makers to be both invaluable and inspirational: "It's great to have similar minded people to bounce ideas off and network with."

Robin & Rose specialises in a range of affordable items sourced worldwide, with an emphasis on products from smaller, independent designers. These products sit alongside Maggie's own designs and creations.

For people thinking of starting a business, the issue of product pricing can be a difficult one, but Maggie wanted to get to grips with this early on: "Ensure you cost your products properly, including your time to make them and this allows you to work out your retail price."

Maggie is looking at ways to expand the business and is putting the finishing touches to a premium range of candles which she hopes to wholesale.

"The aim is to allow me to make my part-time hobby into a full-time career, which would be amazing!"

**TOP TIP!** *"Stay positive at all times even on the bad days!"*

❀ **www.robinandrose.com**

❀ **www.etsy.com/shop/robinandroseboutique**

❀ **www.facebook.com/robinandrose**

❀ **@robinandrose**

# SALES VIA YOUR OWN SITE

You've started making sales via platform sites and feel it's time to create your own home on the web.

## HOME ON THE WEB, WINDOW TO THE WORLD

Your site is a powerful marketing tool and a way to make money. Having the right technology and knowledge allows you to build, develop and maintain your site. And you can do it all in-house.

Let's look at the main ways to develop a professional looking online presence.

## BLOGGING

Blogging is a website or part of a website that's regularly updated by an individual or a group of 'bloggers'. There are blogs on any number of topics and the fact that anyone can start blogging for free makes the medium diverse and exciting.

It's an easy way to get online, as you write posts on your topic of choice, upload images and video and become the go-to place for customers looking for your advice/tips/products. Search engines love blogs and the more you write, the higher up the search-engine ranks you will go. Writing regularly is likely to lead to a loyal readership and it's an effective way to communicate your news with existing and potential customers.

Readers can add their comments to your entries if you allow them and you can use your blog to answer questions and establish yourself as an expert in your field. It's free and easy to get started. Try one of the services below.

- Blogger | **www.blogger.com**
- Typepad | **www.typepad.com**
- WordPress | **www.wordpress.com**

### Now you see me

After getting to grips with blogging, why not try your hand at vlogging? This stands for video blogging and is an effective way to interact with customers who want to see you, your products and other happy customers.

# MAKE MONEY FROM YOUR WEBSITE

As traffic to your online home increases, so also do your chances of generating income. Make a profit from with this top ten list of options.

### 1. Display advertising

Offer advertising on your site. The more niche your audience, the more likely you are to attract advertisers. Create a media rate card and include the following information:

❀   number of unique visitors

❀   number of impressions

❀   average duration of visit

❀   visitor demographics.

Upload the rate card to your site and send it to corporate marketing departments and media-buying agencies.

## TIP: SHOW ME YOUR RATES!

*The purpose of a media rate card is to show potential advertisers what your site can deliver to them in terms of traffic and possible sales. To do this, include some key points:*

❀   *A brief description of the site: What it does and for whom.*

❀   *Visitor demographics: Do you have data on the age of your site visitors, their home region, gender, etc? If so, include it, as it helps build a picture of your audience.*

❀   *Site traffic: What are your unique visitor numbers and length of time spent on the site? Include a note or graph if the figures are increasing.*

❀   *Costings: Do you have a cost-per-click (CPC) or cost-per-impression (CPM) rate? If so, include it here, along with the price of other sponsorship options. Offer a menu but leave some flexibility, with 'costed on a project basis' for sponsor features that would benefit from a more tailored proposal.*

❀   *Screenshots: Showing how and where adverts or sponsored features appear on the site.*

❀   *Media activity: Note where you've recently been covered in the media, online and off, so that potential sponsors can see how and where you're promoting the site.*

❀ *Testimonials: Positive comments from existing sponsors give credibility to you and confidence to the next potential sponsor.*

❀ *Team details: Who are the faces behind the site and what are their credentials? In other words, your background career and activities, etc.*

*Round this off with your contact details so that anyone interested can get in touch and place an order!*

## 2. Google AdSense

This tool from Google does the work for you in that it places relevant ads on your site and earns you money when people click on them. You can customise the appearance of the ads so they sit well with the style of your site.

❀ **www.google.co.uk/adsense**

## 3. TextLinkAds

These ads offer direct click-throughs from text on your site. You submit your site to TextLinkAds and then upload the ad code provided. It's your choice whether you approve or deny the supplied ads. Once that's done, you start making money as visitors click on the ads. Try this and Skimlinks, which converts words on your site to affiliate links so that you earn from those, too.

❀ TextLinkAds | **www.text-link-ads.com**

❀ Skimlinks | **www.skimlinks.com**

## 4. Sponsored conversations

Get paid for posts (and now tweets) with services like IZEA that match bloggers with advertisers. Some doubt the ethical stance of paying a blogger to write something about a product but there's no doubt that it's a moneymaker.

❀ **www.izea.com**

## 5. Affiliate schemes

Sign up to affiliate schemes like the Amazon Associates programme, where you can earn up to 10% in referrals by driving traffic to Amazon through specially formatted links. You earn referral fees on sales generated through those links. Monthly cheques are sent to you from Amazon and it's easy and free to join.

❀ **affiliate-program.amazon.co.uk**

## 6. Sponsored features

This could include a host of options. Approach advertisers with suggestions of a sponsored eBook, e-news, podcast, webchat, poll or survey. These applications can be added to your site at a low cost yet generate good revenue. See page 139 for details on how these features can help you become an expert in your field. For:

❀ eBook creation, try Blurb (**www.blurb.com**)

❀ a survey or poll feature, try SurveyMonkey (**www.surveymonkey.com**)

❀ email marketing, try MailChimp (**www.mailchimp.com**)

## 7. Expert help

Offer your expertise and charge people to log on and watch or listen. This could be made available through:

❀ Teleclasses: Invite customers and contacts to a call where you offer your expertise on a one-to-many basis.

❀ Webinars: Deliver a presentation to potentially thousands of paying customers via GoToWebinar (**www.gotowebinar.co.uk**).

## 8. Deals with suppliers

Do deals with suppliers. Hosting a travel blog? Agree a percentage each time a booking is made via your site. Hosting a shedworking blog? Create a directory that includes all garden office suppliers but with an enhanced listing for those who pay.

## 9. Turn a blog into a book

Turn blog posts into a bestselling book! Contact Enterprise Nation with ideas and proposals in this area as we could be interested in publishing you!

## 10. Please donate

If you'd rather just ask for a small donation from your visitors, this is possible too via a donate feature from PayPal. Add a PayPal donate button to your site: **tinyurl.com/63swy9x**

# YOUR OWN WEBSITE

Create a home on the web through having your own website that you have built to your own requirements or by investing in a template website. Let's look at both options.

## DIY

You have decided to build your own site (or have a developer take care of it for you). The first thing to do is buy a domain, i.e. a URL. A domain makes up a part of your website and email address. For example, the domain name I own is enterprisenation.com. My website address is www.enterprisenation.com and my email address is emma@enterprisenation.com. Both use the enterprisenation.com domain name.

A domain isn't only your web address, it's also a big part of your brand on the internet so think carefully when choosing one – although your options will be increasingly limited, since so many combinations have already been snapped up!

There are lots of domain registration companies whose websites allow you to check for available domain names and often suggest available alternatives. Here are three options.

❀ 1&1 | **www.1and1.co.uk**

❀ 123-reg | **www.123-reg.co.uk**

❀ Easily | **www.easily.co.uk**

Registering a domain name doesn't give you a website, just an address for it (and an email address). Think of it like reserving a car parking space. You've got the space, now you need to buy the car!

A hosting company will sort you out with the web space to host your website. This is measured in megabytes and gigabytes, just like the information on your computer.

You upload the files that make up a website – pictures and pages – to this space, so that the rest of the world can see them.

In terms of how much web space you will need, basic hosting packages offer about 250MB of web space, but anything over 1 or 2GB is more sensible and it will also allow you to handle more traffic on your website as it grows more popular.

With a domain name and web space, potential customers should be able to type your website address into their browser and find out all about your business – just as soon as you've built your site. Finding a hosting company shouldn't be hard. Most domain registration companies, including those mentioned above, offer web space as a package and vice versa.

When it comes to hiring a designer, have a think about what you'd like your website to do for your business. The easiest way to start is to think of your website as a brochure, but remember to include the following pages at the very least.

❀ About us

❀ News

❀ Products or services

❀ FAQs (Frequently Asked Questions)

❀ Contact us

Choose a designer who has carried out work you like the look of for companies in a similar kind of sector to your own. That way, the designer will understand what site you're after – and what your kind of visitor will be looking for, as well as how they like to browse and buy. Check out sites like the Enterprise Nation Directory (**www.enterprisenation.com**) to find the right web designer for you.

See page 106 for details on how to integrate PayPal payments into your site and turn site content into commerce.

### Template site

If DIY feels and sounds too much like hard work, there are a good number of companies offering template websites that come with domain registration, hosting, e-commerce and a basic level of design as part of the package.

There are a number of template site providers offering websites that can be set up today and trading by tomorrow. Check out these options:

❀ Moonfruit | **www.moonfruit.com**

❀ Create | **www.create.net**

❀ Magento | **www.magentocommerce.com**

❀ SupaDupa | **www.supadupa.me**

---

**TIP: TAKE CARE OF THE TS AND CS**

*When building your site, include some basic terms and conditions. These will cover information about the site content and your policy on data privacy. View sample terms and conditions on the Business Link website:* **bit.ly/csYSTz**

---

# E-COMMERCE TOOLS

Open your website up to sales by adding a shopping cart or plugging in an e-commerce tool. Here are some suggestions.

### Shopping carts

Add a shopping cart to make life easy for your visitors to click and buy. Check out these shopping cart providers:

- ❀ GroovyCart | **www.groovycart.co.uk**
- ❀ Zen Cart | **www.zen-cart.com**
- ❀ RomanCart | **www.romancart.com**
- ❀ osCommerce | **www.oscommerce.com**
- ❀ CubeCart | **www.cubecart.com**
- ❀ Frooition | **www.frooition.com**

Research the product that suits you best, taking into account hosting provision, back-end admin, and built-in search engine optimisation.

## Plugging in

If you are blogging and want to start selling, consider these plug-in tools that could turn browsers into buyers:

- ❀ WordPress e-Commerce shopping cart | **bit.ly/fEgQHo**
- ❀ PayPal Shortcodes – insert PayPal buttons in your posts or pages | **bit.ly/eUjhgM**
- ❀ View a complete list of WordPress e-commerce plugins | **bit.ly/eTEkwZ**

Many e-commerce platform sites come with an in-built payment system. Here are the main ones:

## PayPal

Regarded as the leading international payment platform, PayPal has more than 84 million active registered accounts and is available in 190 markets, meaning you can successfully trade in all these markets!

For online store owners, PayPal is easy to introduce and offers customers peace of mind that payment will be secure. Indeed, PayPal's total payment volume in 2009 represented nearly 15% of global e-commerce.

The company offers three main products: website payments standard, website payments pro, and express checkout. To enable your customers to buy multiple items, use a free PayPal shopping cart. Your customers then click the button to make a purchase.

✤ Add PayPal button | **bit.ly/blxrUn**

With PayPal, there are no set-up charges, monthly fees or cancellation charges, and fee levels vary depending on the volume of sales.

✤ **www.paypal.co.uk**

## Google Wallet

Google Wallet is a global payment system. There are no set-up charges and fees depend on the volume of your sales. With monthly sales of less than £1,500, the fee is currently 3.4% plus 20p per transaction. This transaction fee decreases in line with sales volumes increasing.

✤ **checkout.google.co.uk**

## Sage Pay

Sage Pay is a card payment service that allows you to accept payments by PayPal and major debit and credit cards. It is simple to manage and easy to integrate within your website. The fee is £20 per month for merchants processing up to 1,000 transactions per quarter and 10p per transaction for merchants processing more than 1,000 transactions per quarter, with a minimum charge of £20 per month. There are no set-up fees, no percentage fees and no annual charges.

✤ **www.sagepay.com**

## TIP: JUST-IN-TIME PAYMENT

*Adding a PayPal payment button to your site will enable you to accept payment from all major credit and debit cards, as well as bank accounts, around the world. You can set it up in less than 15 minutes.*

*For more information on e-commerce, view the video series '10 steps to e-commerce success' produced by Enterprise Nation in association with PayPal:* **bit.ly/gEdpWO**

# DISTANCE SELLING REGULATIONS

One thing to bear in mind when selling goods to consumers via the internet, mail order or by phone, is compliance with the Consumer Protection (Distance Selling) Regulations 2000. The key features of the regulations are:

❀ You must offer consumers clear information including details of the goods offered, delivery arrangements and payment, the supplier's details and the consumer's cancellation right before they buy (known as prior information). This information should be provided in writing.

❀ The consumer has a period of seven working days from delivery of the items to cancel their contract with you.

❀ These regulations only apply when selling to consumers, as opposed to businesses. In the event of a contract being ceased, you have to refund money, including delivery charges, within 30 days of the date of cancellation.

For more guidance, see **tinyurl.com/63798kq**.

Keep customers coming back with offers and good service and attract new customers by making some noise and rising up the search engine ranks!

Charity Nichols has succeeded in making sales via her own site as well as through a physical store. Both have contributed to the company's success . . .

# MONEY MAKER

**NAME:** Charity Nichols

**TALENT:** Retailer

**BUSINESS:** Green Tulip

CHARITY NICHOLS began her entrepreneurial journey in 2006, after leaving John Lewis where she had worked for 14 years in various jobs including buying.

> "We were living in Surrey and I was commuting into London three days a week – which was fine when the children were at nursery but was about to get more complicated as my oldest was due to start school. So we made the big decision to leave Surrey and move down to Wiltshire, where I grew up, and that was the push I needed to start my own business."

Having been in retail, Charity knew she wanted to set up a retail business but the challenge was finding the right niche and making it work. Her business, Green Tulip, came out of the enjoyment of finding the perfect gift for friends and family, together with Charity's personal beliefs for ethical and sustainable living.

> "My husband lived in Japan in the early 90s and they were recycling even then (when in the UK we were still throwing wine bottles in the bin – what a horrifying thought now!). As a result, as a family we were very aware of minimising our impact on the planet but as a born and bred shopper I still wanted nice, stylish products."

Green Tulip began with a 'soft launch' in the autumn of 2006 and Charity found those first few months a steep learning curve.

"I remember spending days preparing for the first trade fair at our local school – laying everything out on the table in our conservatory and printing out little price cards for everything. On the day I took two carloads of stock over, set up the stand – and took under £100! I went on to do five other fairs leading up to Christmas and each time I learnt something new – and took less stock and more money!"

At the same time, Charity was working with a friend on plans to open a shop on a farm site near their house. After a couple of months, they opened The Inner Yard (**www.theinneryard.co.uk**) and are still there five years later!

That summer, the Green Tulip website was also launched.

"I spent a lot of late nights photographing, writing copy and uploading product information. I remember being very excited when the website went live on 23 July – and then nothing happened! Our first order finally arrived on 19th September – a very exciting moment!"

The Inner Yard shop depends on word of mouth to promote it due to its location.

"It is hard work getting people into the shop but once they find us they are back regularly and the business has grown steadily over the last five years. I remember a customer coming in once and saying she heard about us in the changing rooms at a nearby leisure centre!"

To promote the business, Charity looked for professional help fairly early on.

"I started working with a PR representative and she has been a real support over the last five years. I decided to use a local person rather than a big company and got a great service. We meet regularly to look at what's new and she is an enthusiastic fan of the products, which I definitely think helps when she is talking about us to the magazines. We've had some great press over the years (including having products featured in *Country Living, Good Food* and the *Telegraph* and *Times* Saturday magazines) and clearly see a spike in sales when certain products are featured. We also have a press page on our website showing all our coverage which I think helps give customers confidence that we are a well-respected and trustworthy business."

Search engine optimisation (SEO) and social media also play a key role in promoting the brand.

"I started working with an SEO consultant a few years ago and that has helped grow sales on the website. I take a lot of advice on which search data to add to the site and the consultant keeps me up to date with the latest thinking in the web world!

The final bit of the promotion jigsaw is social media which I am finally getting into! We have a Facebook page and have just started on Twitter. I've also got a Pinterest account and like to think I was quite an early adopter on that one!

I think it is really important to make the content interesting and personal rather than just a sales feed. It's a great way of helping customers understand what your brand is all about."

When Green Tulip started, Charity did everything – all the sourcing, uploading the products, packing the boxes and queuing at the post office! As the business has grown, she has taken on a small team who work with her on the website.

"I still do all the sourcing and check all of the copy going onto the website though – after all it is vital that Green Tulip retains the principles at its heart."

So what is in store for Green Tulip in the future?

"I have so many ideas and just not enough hours in the day – a typical small business owner! Only half of the products I sell in the shop are on the website so we are working hard to upload all the new ranges. For example, I sell cards really well in the shop so would love to have a little 'card shop' on the website (all printed on recycled or sustainable paper of course!). I also want to put together some themed gift baskets for Christmas and I know we could make up great sets by bringing together some of the ranges we stock. In short, there's plenty to do!"

**TOP TIP!** *"Be open-minded about how your business is developing and where it will go in the future. I've certainly never regretted trying things and I know my business wouldn't be where it is today if I hadn't been flexible about where the business was going."*

❀ **www.greentulip.co.uk**

❀ **www.facebook.com/greentulipuk**

❀ **@ethicalgifts**

❀ **www.pinterest.com/greentulipuk**

❀ **www.theinneryard.co.uk**

❀ **www.facebook.com/theinneryard**

# 5 SALES TIPS FOR THE CRAFT INDUSTRY

JACKIE WADE, MD of Winning Sales and author of *Successful Selling for Small Business* gives her top five tips for face-to-face sales success . . .

**1.** Think of selling in the positive and good old-fashioned context of 'sales assistant'. You don't have to be pushy, aggressive or in-your-face to be successful at selling. You need to focus instead on helping or assisting your customers to buy well and hopefully that means buy you.

**2.** Seek to engage with your potential customers. Smile, be warm and friendly and above all be natural. Be you.

**3.** Don't be aloof or put physical barriers in the way. If you're selling on a stall or at an exhibition or standing behind a table or counter, come around and stand next to your customer. Seek to connect through your body language and eye contact.

**4.** Talk to your customers – don't sell at them. Ask them simple things like "How are you enjoying the fair?", "Have you made any interesting purchases so far?" Build rapport, than seek to chat about their specific needs in relation to your product – who's it for, what's the occasion, when is it ... "How can I help you today?"

**5.** Equally, be careful about talking too much or trying to tell them too much about your product. Tell them what they need to know and focus on the key benefits and USPs (unique selling points, i.e. what makes your product or you different).

❀ *Successful Selling for Small Business* |
**www.brightwordpublishing.com/successfulselling**

# CHAPTER SEVEN
## MAKE SOME
## NOISE

**S**ALES are coming in and you want to tell the world about you and your new business. Profile brings new customers, new sales and headlines!

# GETTING KNOWN

Become known in the press and online by making friends with the media, hosting events, entering awards and becoming an expert in your field. Create the right first impression, whether a customer meets you at an event or visits you online. Here's guidance on how to achieve it all. First step: getting known.

## PLOT THE SCRIPT

Imagine yourself as the star of your own Hollywood movie. Are you an action hero, battling against the odds (think James Dyson) or a brand-leading lady (think Nigella Lawson)? Plot the action and write the script. It will help you define your message to the media.

## FIND THE RIGHT CONTACTS

Research the journalists you think are interested in your field. Note their email addresses from the bottom of their articles, follow them on Twitter, get to know them and send them exclusive stories about you and your business.

---

**TIP: FOLLOWING THE MEDIA**

*Follow media contacts and channels on Twitter to pick up on profile opportunities. Here are a few from radio/TV/magazines:*

- *@BBCBreakfast*
- *@BBCOnTheMoney*
- *@talktothepress*
- *@findaTVexpert*
- *@TheTimesLive*
- *@guardian*
- *@PrimaMag*
- *@countrylivinguk*

---

Please contact Enterprise Nation with your story as we are always profiling start-ups and small businesses on our website, in books (like this one!), in kits, in videos and as part of the national StartUp Britain campaign. Submit your story at **www.enterprisenation.com.**

# WRITE A RELEASE

Writing a press release costs nothing but your time, yet it can generate thousands of pounds worth of publicity. If you're emailing a press release to journalists, write the text in the body of the email and include it in an attachment, too.

Your press release should have an attention-grabbing headline, the main facts in the first sentence and evidence and quotes from as high-profile people and companies as possible in the main body of the text. Include great quality images wherever you can to lift the piece and put a face to the brand (but don't make the email file size huge!). You could also use a press-release distribution service to secure wider exposure. My personal favourite is ResponseSource (**www.responsesource.com**) but there's also PR Newswire (**www.prnewswire.co.uk**) and PRWeb (**www.prweb.com**). If you don't get a response, follow up!

---

**TIP: LINK REQUEST**

*If you're being featured online ask the journalist if they can include a link to your site. That way, readers can be on your site within a click.*

---

# 5 TIPS FOR TOP PR

GREG SIMPSON, founder and director of Press For Attention and author of *The Small Business Guide to PR*, gives his top five tips for building a successful PR campaign . . .

### 1. Have a 'cunning plan'

Too many people rush into PR and marketing campaigns with no real plan. Think:

❀ What are the goals of the campaign?

❀ How do you want to come across in terms of tone?

❀ Key messages – what do you want to get across?

❀ Strategy – consider how various companies get their messages across.

❀ Tactics – PR stunts, press releases, controversy, photo opportunities, comment/opinion pieces, debates, flash mobs, press trips, celebrity endorsements, competitions.

There are so many ways to get noticed. Blend them to your requirements and skills.

## 2. Research your customer/audience

There is little point getting a full article page in Dog Grooming Monthly if you sell organic ice cream to boutique hotels! Find out who your ideal customer is and research what they read, listen to and watch. Then, REALLY take the time to read the publications and get to know what sort of stories they publish.

## 3. Find the news hook

Be honest, is your story really news? Examples include: new products, new staff, new promotions, new premises, anniversaries, company expansion, financial milestones and charity efforts.

You can also provide topical comment on a newsworthy subject. Keep an eye out for issues that affect your business or your customers. This takes practice and you need to establish credibility in your subject area first. Consider starting a blog that provides regular, lively and informed comment in your area of expertise to build your profile. I use WordPress, which is free.

## 4. Got a story?

Great! Now you need a SIMPLE press release for a journalist to refer to. People worry that their efforts don't sound flashy enough to warrant attention but you aren't aiming for a Booker Prize, you are aiming for coherent and interesting NEWS.

Use "Who, What, When, How and Why?" as a framework and imagine yourself as the journalist. Is this definitely of interest to their readers? Is it simple enough to understand? Does it stand up on its own?

I would stick to a maximum of 300 words and keep the press release focused on the news angle.

## 5. Hit them between the eyes

Journalists get hundreds of press releases every day. Ensure that the headline and first paragraph sum up the entire story in a nutshell. Ideally, your press release should still make sense even if an editor dropped two or three paragraphs.

I call the journalist beforehand to outline my story. This helps iron out any creases and demonstrates that you are trying to work with them and their audience.

*More tips can be found on Greg's website* **www.pressforattention.com** *and his book is available from* **www.brightwordpublishing.com/products/view/865858**

---

### TIP: AN IMAGE SPEAKS LOUDER THAN WORDS

*When a picture speaks a thousand words you can afford to talk less! Consider hiring a professional photographer to take pictures of you and your work. Maybe you can do this as a barter deal? Pick up your own digital camera and do it yourself or contact your local college and ask if any photography students would like to offer their time so you receive a free image and the student has material for their portfolio. A journalist is much more likely to cover your story if you have great imagery to go with it. Use the images on your website and in promotion materials and let your business speak for itself.*

# ENTER AWARDS

Enter awards and competitions and enjoy the press coverage that goes with them. Many award schemes are free to enter and are targeted at start-up businesses. Writing the entry will help to clarify your goals and vision, and winning will bring profile and prizes.

To find out about upcoming awards, visit StartUp Britain (**www.startupbritain.org**) and Awards Intelligence (**www.awardsintelligence.co.uk**) or check out the following:

- ❀ *Country Living* Magazine Kitchen Table Talent Awards: If you're working on a talent or skill from the kitchen table and know it can be turned into a business, this competition is for you. Prizes include office equipment, profile in the magazine and advice/support from business experts!
  **www. kitchentabletalent.com**

- ❀ Shell LiveWIRE Grand Ideas Awards: Up to four awards per month of £1,000 for anyone aged 16 to 30 looking to get an idea off the ground.
  **www.shell-livewire.org/awards**

- ❀ The Pitch: Enter regional heats and pitch to experienced judges for a place in the national finals. Takes place across the UK
  **www.thepitchuk.com**

- ❀ Social Enterprise Awards: Celebrates social enterprises of all ages.
  **www.socialenterprise.org.uk/events/social-enterprise-awards-1**

- ❀ Nectar Small Business Awards: Offers cash prizes and plenty of Nectar points!
  **www.nectar.com/business-sba2012**

- ❀ Startups Awards: Celebrating small businesses of all shapes and sizes
  **www.startupsawards.co.uk**

# HOST AN EVENT

Invite the press to come and meet you. This doesn't have to be an expensive affair; the secret is partnering with others who would benefit from being in front of your audience. Approach a venue and ask if they would host at no cost in exchange for the venue receiving profile. Do the same with caterers. Then give invited guests a reason to attend – have a theme, an interesting speaker, a launch announcement, anything that will grab their attention and encourage them to attend.

Make use of free online services such as Eventbrite (**www.eventbrite.com**) or Meetup (**www.meetup.com**) to send out invites and receive RSVPs.

## TIP: I'M A CELEBRITY. GET ME ON YOUR PRODUCT!

*One way to attract profile and attention is to have a celebrity endorse your product or service. Amanda Frolich has seen the benefit of this having endorsements from celebrity clients such as Victoria Beckham and Catherine Tate, with a section dedicated on her website to their glowing testimonials . . .*

# MONEY MAKER

**NAME**: Amanda Frolich

**TALENT**: Educating pre-school children through fun, fitness and music

**BUSINESS**: Amanda's Action Club

AMANDA FROLICH began researching the idea for her business in 1990, but it wasn't until 1998 that Amanda's Action Club was created and began to take off.

> "I remember completing a music and movement course and thinking this is just what kids need! Nobody was doing interactive mums and toddler's classes that were exciting at the time so I thought there could be a gap in the market. And it turned out there was."

To kick things off, Amanda hired a local community hall, printed some leaflets and put them up in local shop windows. She also put an ad in the newspaper and told everyone she knew what she was doing.

> "I started with just a few mums and kids to begin with, but it soon grew as word spread that I had created something a bit different."

The business has since grown and Amanda has a team to help promote the business, including a PR agent and SEO expert. Amanda's Action Club features in forums such as Netmums and Nappyvalley as well as in *Families* magazines and in the NCT booklet. They also market online, send newsletters to their customer database, use social media, direct marketing and offer competitions to their fans.

Despite embracing new technology and social media, Amanda continues with the more traditional form of leaflet mailouts to drum up interest in the classes.

"We do regular leaflet drops in the areas local to our classes – it's not hi-tech but it works!"

For Amanda, a key part of keeping customers satisfied is to keep the brand fresh and evolve so children get the very best entertainment possible.

"Every month we get our staff together for retraining; we prance about, get creative and come up with new ideas. It's just hard work and a lot of passion, really. We're always thinking about how we can make things better and give more value."

Amanda has expanded the business and taken on several members for her team.

"I stick to what I'm good at and hire great people to do the rest. I'm very social and have a wide network so it's never too hard to find the right people."

So what does Amanda have in store for the future?

"I've always had big dreams for Amanda's Action Club. I think our brand of entertainment is incredibly beneficial for young children's development so naturally I want to see it spread as widely as possible. We're exploring the possibility of working in Dubai and Palm Beach and Miami in Florida too.

"Our national franchise scheme is launching this year so that will be crucial to our international development, and we're in the process of creating an animated character – a little girl superhero – to represent the brand and inspire children to stay active. Watch this space!"

**TOP TIP!** *"Believe in yourself and don't ever give up!"*

- ❀ www.amandasactionclub.co.uk

- ❀ www.facebook.com/amandasactionclub

- ❀ @actionamanda

# JOIN A GROUP OR CLUB

Signing up to a local business club or network is good for business and your social life. You get together to do deals but also end up making friends. Check out these national business networks to find your natural fit:

- ❀ 1230 TWC – events for women in business
  **www.1230.co.uk**

- ❀ 4Networking – national network of business breakfast groups
  **www.4networking.biz**

- ❀ The Athena Network – networking organisation for women in business
  **www.theathenanetwork.com**

- ❀ Business Scene – hosts regional and national networking events as well as hosting an online directory of over 10,000 events across the UK
  **www.business-scene.com**

- ❀ Ecademy – national site with local and regional meet-ups
  **www.ecademy.com**

- ❀ School for Startups – headed by serial entrepreneur Doug Richard, School for Startups travels the UK hosting events for anyone considering starting a business. Gems from Doug's presentations are broadcast via S4STV.
  **www.schoolforcreativestartups.com**

❀ Women in Rural Enterprise (WiRE) – networking and business club for rural women in business
**www.wireuk.org**

❀ First Friday Network – a free business networking event held monthly; informal gatherings in a welcoming environment
**www.firstfriday-network.co.uk**

❀ StartUp Saturday – a monthly class hosted by Enterprise Nation that not only offers instruction on how to start a business but also ensures a ready-made support group for anyone wishing to become their own boss.
**www.enterprisenation.com/events/startup-saturday-2012**

There are also chambers, associations, trade groups and enterprise agencies that host regular events:

❀ British Chambers of Commerce | **www.britishchambers.org.uk**

❀ Federation of Small Businesses (FSB) | **www.fsb.org.uk**

❀ Forum of Private Business | **www.fpb.org**

❀ National Enterprise Network | **www.nationalenterprisenetwork.org**

National bodies that hold events and offer support at certain stages in your entrepreneurial career include:

❀ NACUE (**www.nacue.com**) – national organisation that represents university-based enterprise societies across the UK and hosts events to encourage student entrepreneurship.

❀ PRIME (**www.prime.org.uk**) (The Prince's Initiative for Mature Enterprise) – a network for the over 50s that provides free information, events and training.

From attending events you may meet businesses with whom there is a shared opportunity. Denise Rawls credits networking and being part of business clubs as a key factor in the success of her business . . .

# MONEY MAKER

**NAME**: Denise Rawls

**TALENT**: Cardmaking

**BUSINESS**: Strange Fruit

DENISE RAWLS had thought about starting a greeting card company reflective of people of colour for years but had not yet turned the idea into a business. When she got married and had her son, she was disappointed not to receive any cards from her friends and family that she could identify with. So in October 2009 she decided to stop thinking and start up. Strange Fruit launched a year later.

After deciding she was going to go for it, Denise knew she needed to get her cards out to the general public.

> "I walked into an independent store in an upmarket part of London, showed the buyer my first collection and asked if they would like to stock the cards. They said yes!"

Spurred on by this, and with the thought that her cards would appeal to black professionals, Denise began to approach shops where she thought her customers might shop. "Turns out I was wrong," she says. "My cards are bought by people of all ethnic backgrounds simply because they like them. Being stocked at the Mary Portas shops within House of Fraser is testament to that."

Following on from her progress in getting local shops to stock the cards, Denise thinks meeting buyers and attending trade shows has been good for her business, as is social media.

"On a day-to-day level because I still have my day job I rely on social media to stay in touch with my customers and supporters because it's quick, easy and free. The odd chat on the radio or mention in a paper is great too. I have found all my customers like to chat and understand the concept behind the business. They then tell other people and the cards get lots of word of mouth recommendations."

Denise believes networking has played a part in the success of her business.

"I try to attend at least one networking event a month, I give away freebies or little extras and I think most of all I don't try and sell to people all the time; 'if they like it they will buy' is my philosophy – people just need to know my cards exist."

As a result of Denise's hard work, Strange Fruit has gone global!

"I decided to focus on getting an overseas agent, so I did some research on companies that represent other boutique greeting card companies in America and approached three by email. One really liked my range and I have licensed ten designs to them. My cards were at the National Stationery Show in New York and the next step is promoting the cards myself to the American market and then looking for another agent in another country."

In order to achieve this, Denise is planning to take on another member of staff.

"I need to take someone on because I'm launching a range of invitations for birthdays, baby showers and hen parties, and working on my first custom wedding stationery collection, which is really exciting!"

Her advice to anyone thinking of giving it a go? Just do it!

"I put off starting Strange Fruit because I didn't have any time, any money or any experience of the greeting card industry, and I had no idea how to use Photoshop. When I made the decision to start the company, I read as much as I could about the industry and learnt what I needed to know about photo editing software and took it one step at a time.

The only thing that changed was my attitude because I wanted to make a difference and wanted my son and other children of colour to be able to have a birthday card they could identify with."

**TOP TIP!** *"Figure out what steps you need to take and find a way to take them. Starting small means I have learnt as I have gone along, not incurred any debt and been able to adapt the business quickly when I have found a better way of doing something."*

❀ **www.ilovestrangefruit.com**

❀ **@ilvstrangefruit**

# ATTEND TRADE SHOWS

Promote your brand by attending the shows your customers attend. Craft fairs and shows are excellent places to sell products, meet customers and get your business in front of the ideal target audience. See the next page for trade show and fairs tips and techniques!

## Shows and fairs: the perfect sales and marketing opportunity

Start by deciding on the type of fair or event you want to exhibit at, i.e. where your customers are likely to be. Then look at location – is the show out of town, meaning hotel and transport costs and, if so, are there ways you could reduce your expenditure, for example staying with friends, or sharing costs with another business?

Search online and talk to peers to find out the best fairs/events/shows to attend and keep updated with blogs and websites for mention of the more popular events. Don't forget your local shops and newsletters/magazines as these are often a source of useful information.

Confident you've found the right event, look at how much exhibition space you'll need and can afford. Look carefully at what is included in the exhibition price/space – will they provide a table and chairs, electricity, an internet connection? Most events will have an online or paper application process; be clear about what you make and sell – the organisers may have thousands of people applying for space so make their decision as easy as possible. Once happy with your application form, press send and wait! It may take a couple of days before you receive confirmation.

## You've been accepted!

If you have been accepted for the event, congratulations!

There will be lots to do to get you ready to exhibit so here are some key points to start with:

❀ Make a list of what you have in stock – do you have enough of each product to take with you, or will you need to produce some extra stock? How will you price these items, and will you be displaying prices on them, or will you have a clear price list which people can refer to? Will you be running special offers at the event?

❁ Your exhibition space will need to be decorated – think about sourcing items and backdrops that will highlight your brand and your message, and show off products to their best advantage. For example, do you sell handmade rings? Instead of having them laid flat in a box, could you display them on a hand mannequin or use a prop to dangle them from? If you sell clothing, do you need to take a mirror? These little things can make the difference between someone buying your product or walking away. Think about stalls you have visited when you've been at craft fairs and the ones that stood out to you – can you take inspiration from them to create your own stand?

❁ Don't forget marketing materials, such as business cards, flyers and special offer leaflets. Do you have these ready or will you need to produce them? Do you have anything you can use as a handout to passers-by? Do you also have a way of taking potential customers' contact details?

❁ Packaging materials – ensure you have enough to last you for the entire event. If you wrap your products up, it could be a nice idea to invest in some stickers with your logo and website details to seal the package, so that when the customer gets home they remember you and your stall and may be tempted to buy again. You could even look at customised carrier bags – extra advertising as your customers wander around.

❁ Ahead of the event, ask organisers how the drop-off and delivery process works so you have enough time to set up your stall and get yourself ready before customers begin to arrive and you're out of the venue by the correct time once the event finishes.

❁ Consider whether you need public liability insurance to display your products or, for example, to have public food demonstrations.

Another important point to be considered is how you will take payment. Most people will want to pay by cash or credit/debit card so think about how you will offer this.

## Cash

Accepting cash is fairly straightforward. All you'll need to do is set up a small float to provide change and some way of recording sales. The float doesn't have to be enormous – look at the prices you are selling your products for and plan accordingly (round numbers are easiest to deal with). It is a good idea to take along a receipt book so that you can write out receipts for anyone paying cash.

An inventory list will also be invaluable here as this will enable you to keep track of what stock is selling – useful for evaluating sales after the fair and also to keep you on top of what stock is remaining.

## Credit/debit cards

Many people nowadays will expect to be able to pay for goods via credit or debit card, so it is a good idea to be able to offer this payment method if you can. After all, you don't want to miss out on sales because you aren't able to take payment. Accepting card payments is more complicated than accepting cash and it might mean that you have to pay a small fee but it will be beneficial in the long run.

One of the ways you can accept payment is through WorldPay.

### *WorldPay*

WorldPay is one of the UK's leading payment services provider, and as part of their service they offer mobile payment terminals which are ideal for events and trade shows, meaning you can take card payments directly from your stall as long as a GPRS mobile phone signal can be received.

You will need to set up a merchant account, which is a bank account specifically for processing credit and debit card orders. More information on how to do that can be found on the Business Link website: **tinyurl.com/6jhy2yy**

The main benefit of the mobile terminal is that it is flexible, accepting all major credit and debit cards, which is a big plus when selling at events, and you can also arrange short-term hire – great for an event or trade show. The terminal is also chip and PIN compliant, capable of producing receipts for you to give you to your customer and also an end of day reconciliation report so that you can see all of the transactions throughout the show.

Your WorldPay merchant account is credited with the value of the card transaction, normally within four working days. WorldPay will send you a merchant statement which details the transactions processed, and how much you've paid for each transaction in fees.

The cost for the transactions currently breaks down as follows:

- Set-up fee: One-time fee for the set-up of your payment gateway is £200.

- Transaction fees: For UK debit cards it's 50p per transaction. On other transactions, you pay 4.5% of the value. You will also pay a charge for the hire of the card terminal.

### PayPal

PayPal recently launched PayPal Mobile, which allows you to send and receive payments via your mobile phone. The new PayPal app is free to download and is then ready to go. Once at the fair, all your customers need to do is to log in to their PayPal account and send you the money for their purchases using the email address tied to your PayPal account. Alternatively, if they also have the PayPal app, you can simply bump your phones together to transfer the information using their new software!

More information on Paypal Mobile can be found at: **www.paypal-marketing.co.uk/ mobile**

## Tradeshow top tips

*Before the event*

❀ Negotiate a good deal – if you're prepared to wait it out, the best deals on stands can be had days before the event is starting. The closer the date, the better the price you'll negotiate as the sales team hurry to get a full house. However, you will need to be fully prepared in terms of stock and your marketing materials.

❀ Tell people you're going – circulate news that you'll be at the event through online networks (giving your location or stand number) and issue a press release if you're doing something newsworthy at the event, maybe launching a new product, having a guest appearance, running a competition, etc.

*At the event*

❀ Be clear on the offer – determine what you are selling and let this be consistent across show materials; from pop-up stands to flyers. Be creative with the stand to keep costs low. Consider offering a supply of mouth-watering refreshments!

❀ Be friendly and approachable – walk around the stall, talk to people and maybe even wear or hold something that you have made and are selling – this could be a conversation starter and seeing the product on a person can make a difference. Let people know about the materials you've used or the particular way the product has been made – engage, engage, engage!

❀ Collect data – find ways to collect attendees' names and details. Offer a prize in exchange for business cards or take details in exchange for a follow-up information pack or offer. Some events also offer the facility to scan the details from the delegates' badges (for a fee).

❀ Take friends/family – invite a supportive team. If you're busy talking to a potential customer, you'll want others on the stand who can be doing the same (or taking the money!). If there's time, get to know the exhibitors around you.

❀ Be prepared – wear comfortable shoes, bring some spare clothes and pack your lunch; if you're busy there may not be time to buy food and drink!

### After the event

❀ Follow-up – within a couple of days of returning from the show, contact the people who expressed interest so that interest can be turned into sales.

❀ Plan ahead – if the show delivered a good return, contact the organisers and ask to be considered for a speaking slot or higher profile at the next event, and confirm your willingness to be a case study or offer testimonial in any post-show promotion.

## POP IN TO A POPUP!

In July 2012 national campaign StartUp Britain launched a project to help small businesses get onto the High Street through:

❀ PitchUp! – referenced earlier this provides small businesses with an opportunity to pitch to large retailers

❀ PopUp! – fills empty shops with small businesses – just like yours!

The first PopUp shop opened in Richmond and there are plans for more. The way it works is a small number of businesses trade in the shop for two weeks at a time and crowdfund the rent (in Richmond the cost is £135 for two weeks trading). As a business owner, you get a shopfront for two weeks and the opportunity to develop new skills as you meet with and sell to customers face-to-face. It's an ideal route to research the market and discover if a permanent store is the right way to go for your business.

❀ StartUp High Street | **www.startupbritain.org/highstreet**

# CRAFT FAIRS, USEFUL LINKS AND RESOURCES

❀ *Prima* Homemade Show
**www.allaboutyou.com/prima/prima-events/craft_event**

❀ *Country Living* Magazine Spring and Christmas Fairs
**www.countrylivingfair.com** | **@CLFairs**

❀ Events listing via UK Handmade
**www.ukhandmade.co.uk/events**

❀ Directory of shops selling handmade goods
**www.ukhandmade.co.uk/shopdirectory** | **@ukhandmade**

## Local events

❀ UK Handmade | **www.ukhandmade.co.uk/localgroups**

❀ Suffolk Craft Society | **www.suffolkcraftsociety.org**

❀ Glasgow Craft Mafia | **www.glasgowcraftmafia.com**

❀ Birmingham Craft Mafia | **www.birminghamcraftmafia.com**

❀ Stitch & Craft Show | **www.stitchandcraft.co.uk**

❀ Farmers' markets, national | **www.localfoods.org.uk**

❀ London Farmers' Markets | **www.lfm.org.uk**

❀ British Sellers on Etsy | **britishsellersonetsy.blogspot.com**

❀ Crafty Fox Market | **craftyfoxmarket.blogspot.com**

❀ Folksy Craft Fair Advice | **blog.folksy.com/category/seller-tips/craft-fair-advice**

❀ Make It, Sell it! day | **www.bl.uk/bipc/workevents/global/friday/makeit.html**

❀ Selvedge | **www.selvedge.org/pages/fair.aspx**

❀ Pick 'n' Mix Makers Market | **picknmixmakersmarket.blogspot.com**

❀ Craft Guerilla | **www.craftguerrilla.com**

❀ Crafts Council | **www.craftscouncil.org.uk/whats-on**

❀ Crafts Magazine | **www.craftscouncil.org.uk/crafts-magazine**

❀ Hello Etsy | **www.helloetsy.com**

❀ Craft directory from the Crafts Council | **www.craftscouncil.org.uk/craft-directory**

## Listing of creative courses

❀ The Design Trust – helps professional designers and craftspeople to create and run better businesses
**www.thedesigntrust.co.uk**

❀ School for Creative StartUps – teaching and supporting creative StartUps
**www.schoolforcreativestartups.com**

❀ From Britain With Love – the guide to buying British
**www.frombritainwithlove.com/directory/creative-courses**

❀ Craft Reactor – a craft collective
**www.craftreactor.com**

# HOW ELSE CAN YOU GET YOUR NAME AND PRODUCTS OUT THERE IN FRONT OF PEOPLE?

## BECOME AN EXPERT

Set yourself up as an expert in your field and the media will come knocking on your door. Do this by writing a book, offering training or developing your own app! Here are eight ways in which you can promote your expertise.

### 1. Publish a book

Become a published author by self-publishing – or approach some of the smaller publishers. Utilise the book as a business development tool, printing on demand to take copies to events, and offering free and downloadable versions to potential customers. Being an author gives you credibility and gives customers information and insight.

❀ Blurb | **www.blurb.com**

❀ Lulu | **www.lulu.com**

❀ Ubyu | **www.ubyubooks.com**

❀ Enterprise Nation Publishing | **www.enterprisenation.com/publishing**

### 2. Present yourself

Put yourself forward to speak at events (consider asking for a fee and/or costs to be covered) or suggest being a satellite speaker, where you are beamed into the conference hall via video link-up, saving the effort and expense of travel. Invite customers and prospects and make the presentation openly available via SlideShare.

❀ SlideShare | **www.slideshare.net**

## 3. Host a webinar

Share your expertise or demonstrate a process by hosting a webinar or visual presentation where a 'live' audience can see you and interact. Achieve this via platforms such as GoToMeeting, GoToWebinar, and WebEx, and remember to host it at a time that suits your target audience.

❀ GoToMeeting | **www.gotomeeting.com**

❀ GoToWebinar | **www.gotowebinar.com**

❀ WebEx | **www.webex.co.uk**

## 4. Produce a film

Maybe the word 'film' is a little ambitious but you can create your own video content with an affordable camcorder or smartphone, or by hiring in a cameraman. Demonstrate your skills or have a sponsored series of guides that can be uploaded to video-sharing sites such as YouTube, Vimeo and eHow, and easily embedded into your site.

❀ YouTube | **www.youtube.com**

❀ Vimeo | **www.vimeo.com**

❀ eHow | **www.ehow.co.uk**

## 5. Broadcast a podcast

For customers who like to listen to what you have to say at a time that suits them, upload a podcast with top tips, interviews and your thoughts of the day. Make it available on your site, iTunes and Podcast Alley to be sure of a wide audience. Follow advice from podcast producer San Sharma on how to record a podcast on a Skype call.

❀ iTunes podcasts | **www.apple.com/itunes/podcasts/specs.html**

❀ Podcast Alley | **www.podcastalley.com**

---

**TIP: HOW TO RECORD A PODCAST ON A SKYPE CALL**

*You can produce a podcast interview using Skype, Pamela Call Recorder, and a little editing know-how. San Sharma, online community manager at Enterprise Nation, shows how it's done, in five simple steps:*

**1.** *Sign up for a free Skype account (***www.skype.com***) and download the Skype software.*

**2.** *If you're using a Windows machine, download Pamela Call Recorder (***www.pamela.biz***), which lets you record your Skype calls. If you're on a Mac, you can download Call Recorder for Skype (***www.ecamm.com***). Both have free trial versions, but only cost around £13 when that's expired.*

**3.** *Call your interviewee using Skype. If they're a Skype user, too, that will be free but if they're on a fixed or mobile line, you'll need to get some Skype Credit (***bit.ly/epymNm***).*

**4.** *Once you've made a connection and agreed with the interviewee the format of the conversation, hit the record button on your call recorder software and you're off!*

**5.** *Edit using Audacity (***audacity.sourceforge.net***), which is free for Windows and Macs, or with GarageBand (***www.apple.com/ilife/garageband***), which comes with most Macs (you can also buy it as part of the iLife package).*

*And the easiest way to share your recording is by uploading it to Audioboo (***www.audioboo.com***), which lets people listen to it on the web, embed on your website or via iTunes or on a mobile phone.*

---

## 6. Deliver training

Whatever your skill, your knowledge could be shared with others. Rather than seeing this as surrendering intelligence to potential competitors, offer instruction you're comfortable with that will create fans and followers who will learn from you, buy from you and, critically, encourage others to do the same. Check out platforms GoToTraining and WebEx, encourage contacts to sign up and then after the demonstration you have a chance to follow up with a group of new contacts.

❀ GoToTraining | **www.gototraining.com**

❀ WebEx Webtraining | **www.webex.co.uk/products/elearning-and-online-training.html**

## 7. Develop an app

Take your content and make an app with a browser-based platform like AppMakr. It's free to use and you can either set a list price to make sales via the App Store or make it available free of charge.

❀ AppMakr | **www.appmakr.com**

## 8. Form groups

Encourage others to discuss, debate and contribute to your content by forming groups utilising social media platforms such as Facebook, LinkedIn and Ning. Bonding interested people to each other will bond them ever closer to you, the content creator and group host.

❀ Facebook | **www.facebook.com**

❀ LinkedIn | **www.linkedin.com**

❀ Ning | **www.ning.com**

**TIP: BE EVERYWHERE**

*Keep in touch with existing customers via a newsletter and reach out to the new by making regular appearances at events, on other people's websites and blogs, in newspapers and magazines, and on radio and TV. Write to the magazines and radio stations that ask people to send in their story. It's a free way to get coverage. The more you're covered, the more you'll be invited to speak and comment, and before you know it, you'll be everywhere!*

# ONLINE PROMOTION

Become well known online and attract customers to your site through search engine optimisation, social tagging and pay-per-click advertising.

## RISE UP THE SEARCH ENGINE RANKS

Search engine optimisation, or SEO, is the process by which you can improve rankings for your website in the top search engines such as Google, so that your site appears on the first few pages of results rather than page 75!

Google uses software known as 'spiders' to crawl the web on a regular basis and find sites to add to its index. There are steps you can take to make it easier for the spiders to find and add your site.

### Start with your homepage

Provide high-quality, text-based content on your pages and regularly add new content – especially on your homepage. If your homepage has useful information and good quality, relevant text, it's more likely to be picked up by the spiders. Beyond the homepage, write pages that clearly describe your topic/service/product. Think about the key words users would type to find your pages and include them on the site.

## Make contributions

Identify influential bloggers and sites in your trade/industry, contact them and offer to write posts. You can also improve your visibility by writing helpful comments in forums and on other people's posts.

## Be well connected

Improve the rank of your site by increasing the number of other high-quality sites that link to your pages; these are referred to as 'inbound links'. For example, if you're running a competition, go to sites that promote competitions and add yours.

You can also register your site with the major search engines:

- ✿ Google | **www.google.co.uk/addurl**
- ✿ Yahoo! | **search.yahoo.com/info/submit.html**
- ✿ Bing | **www.bing.com/webmaster/submitsitepage.aspx**

## TIP: SEARCH ENGINES LOVE LINKS

*Another way to increase your ranking in the search results is to link to other sites and vice versa, but think quality here as opposed to quantity. Sites offering the best 'link juice' are trusted domains, such as news sites, and other popular sites. You could post comments on such sites and blogs and include a link back to your site. Also try these handy hints:*

❀ *Approach sites complementary to your own and suggest reciprocal links.*

❀ *Ensure that your website link is included in all your social media profiles.*

❀ *Register with the major search engines (as explained above).*

❀ *Add your domain to local search services and Google Maps* (**www.google.co.uk/maps**), *Qype* (**www.qype.co.uk**), *Yahoo! Local* (**uk.local.yahoo.com**) *and BView* (**www.bview.co.uk**).

## TAGGING

A webpage's title, referred to as a 'title tag', is part of the SEO mix and can make a difference to your search rankings. It is also the text that appears in the top of the browser window. Include in your title tag your company name and the main key phrase you'd like the search engines to associate with your webpage, keeping it between 60 and 90 characters in length. Duncan Green of Moo Marketing is an SEO expert and explains:

> "The title tag on the homepage for Moo Marketing reads: 'Moo Marketing – Search Engine Marketing – PPC Management – Search Engine Optimisation'; as you can see, the title element is 85 characters long, contains three key phrases and identifies the subject of the webpage."

## PAY-PER-CLICK (PPC) ADVERTISING

The results from your efforts in SEO will appear on the main engines in the central column of the page as a natural or 'organic' search result. But have you spotted results on the right of the page when searching for items yourself? These are paid-for results and referred to as pay-per-click or PPC advertising. PPC is where you pay to have ads displayed when people type in certain words, in the hope it will attract more visitors to your site.

Google AdWords is such a form of PPC advertising. Think of the key words or phrases you think your customers will be searching for and apply them in your Google campaign. Link to your homepage or other pages on the site where you're running a promotion and make the most of geotargeting, which lets you target your ads to specific territories and languages.

You are in full control of the budget and campaign duration.

 **adwords.google.co.uk**

---

### TIP: THINK LIKE A BUYER

*When thinking of the keywords to use in PPC ad campaigns (and in search engine optimisation) think of the words your buyers will be using when searching. Use the Google AdWords Keyword Tool to find the most popular search terms. Apply these words in the campaign and include them in the text on your site.*

---

## SPREAD THE WORD

Make it easy for visitors to spread word of your site through social sharing. Have your site Stumbled, Dugg and Tweeted and make the most of this viral effect. You can add these social bookmarking tools by visiting AddThis (**www.addthis.com**) and choosing the icons you'd like to have displayed on your site.

The most popular are:

- Delicious | **www.delicious.com**
- Digg | **www.digg.com**
- StumbleUpon | **www.stumbleupon.com**
- Twitter | **www.twitter.com**

# THE POWER OF SOCIAL MEDIA

There have never been so many tools at our disposal that we can use to promote our business free of charge, and without a significant outlay of time. I'm talking about social media. It's time to embrace it.

According to research company Nielsen, the world now spends over 110 billion minutes on social networks and blogs per month. This equates to 22% of all time online, or one in every four and half minutes. Embrace this and your business will become known.

Here are the five key tools to use and, crucially, how best to use them.

## 1. Twitter

Visit **www.twitter.com**, create an account, start to follow friends and contacts (and their followers) and get tweeting.

Cost: free

## 2. Facebook

Facebook is the most popular social networking site in the world. The site has over 900 million users worldwide, so if you need to be where your customers are, there's a good chance some of them will be there! You can list on Facebook for free and/or advertise on the site and select an audience based on location, age and interest. Visit **www.facebook.com**, create an account, invite friends and contacts to join your group and get promoting.

Listing cost: free

---

**TIP: FREE GUIDE**

*Download the free 'Boost your Business on Facebook' eBook to make the most of this social platform opportunity:* **www.enterprisenation.com/facebook-book-offer**

---

### 3. LinkedIn

Referring to itself as "the world's largest professional network", LinkedIn has over 100 million members in 200 plus countries. Visit **www.linkedin.com**, create an account and start connecting with existing contacts and finding new ones.

Cost: free (option to upgrade to a business account, which is a paid-for package)

### 4. Flickr

Join **www.flickr.com** and promote yourself visually by uploading photos of you and your products or service, and maybe even a few shots of happy customers. The site also carries video clips so you can show:

- events you host, speak at, or attend
- products you make (the finished product) as well as images of the production process
- happy customers wearing/using/enjoying your products and services
- your workspace
- your family (if you – and they – feel comfortable showing your personal side).
- You can also easily pull the photos into your blog and social media pages.

Cost: free (option to upgrade to a pro account which is a paid-for package)

## 5. YouTube

YouTube is the world's most popular online video community, with 24 hours of video uploaded every minute. Start your own business channel for free, and upload videos profiling you and your work. Create an account (**www.youtube.com/create_account**), start a channel (advice via YouTube video!), and start broadcasting to the world. You can give each of your videos a name and assign keywords to it to help with searching, plus you can have a short description of your company on your profile page. Again, these clips are very easy to add to your website, and they help keep the content fresh and interesting. Footage can even be filmed for free if you have a webcam in your laptop.

Cost: free

**Total budget required for online promotion: £0**

# MEASURE THE RESULTS

Time to measure what's working and what's not. Measure media and press mentions by signing up to Google Alerts (**www.google.co.uk/alerts**) – and you'll be pleased to know there's a whole host of tools that are free to use and will show real-time results for what's working on your site and across social media profiles.

Look out in particular for the sources of your traffic (which are your highest referring sites) and your most popular pages. You can see days where your site receives spikes in visitor levels (and track this back to marketing) and measure if visitors are spending longer periods on the site and which times are popular, e.g. weekends, evenings, lunchtimes, etc. Google Analytics offers intelligence about your website traffic and marketing effectiveness: **www.google.com/analytics**

Other analytics options include:

❀ Alexa – web traffic metrics, site demographics and top URL listings | **www.alexa.com**

- ❀ CrazyEgg – see which pages visitors are visiting with a colourful heat map
  **www.crazyegg.com**

- ❀ Opentracker – gather and analyse web stats and monitor online visitors
  **www.opentracker.net**

- ❀ StatCounter – an invisible web tracker and hit counter that offers data in real time
  **www.statcounter.com**

Hopefully what you will see is an upward curve of visitors and time spent on the site. If you're selling then hopefully this means more sales. And if your site is your business, this means you're in a strong position to attract advertisers and begin doing affiliate deals (see page 101).

Your website is likely to be the first thing potential customers will see of your business – and they'll make their judgement in seconds! Keep it well polished and visitors will soon become customers.

## TIP: A TOP QUALITY IMAGE

*Whether you decide to start online with a blog or a full e-commerce offering, use high-quality royalty-free images on your site and printed materials so that on first click or at first glance, a customer is given a good impression and therefore more likely to buy. Take professional images yourself or consider subscribing to a stock image library such as iStockphoto (***www.istockphoto.com***).*

*Other image libraries include:*

- ❀ *Image Source |* **www.imagesource.com**

- ❀ *Photos.com |* **www.photos.com**

- ❀ *Getty Images |* **www.gettyimages.com**

*Search for creative commons licensed images you can use commercially from Flickr at* **www.compfight.com**.

# FIRST IMPRESSIONS COUNT

In this section we look at how to keep customers coming back and keeping the business in balance as a stepping stone to growth.

## ATTRACT CUSTOMERS BACK

You are making sales via your site and developing a strong community of fans and followers. Give visitors and customers a reason to return by following these steps.

### Fresh and user-generated content

Encourage visitors and customers back to your site with regular posted content, and if it's an e-commerce site, keep the product range updated. Give your site some TLC each day, as fresh content will attract visitors who want to see what's new and also the trawling web spiders who determine search engine results.

Encourage your site visitors to get to know each other through a forum, comment boxes or a plug-in application. Before you know it, a sense of community will develop and visitors will log on each day to find out who's saying what and what's happening with whom.

### Exclusive offers

Extend offers to your existing customers, readers or members that will tempt them back. This offer could be conditional on customers referring a friend: that way your customer returns to the site with others in tow. Add to this with a badge of honour; design an icon that visitors can display on their own site to show their affiliation with you.

## Guest appearances

Invite special guests to appear on your site via guest blog posts, hosting a webchat or a featured interview.

## Keep in touch

Communicate all these good and 'sticky' things to your users through a regular e-newsletter powered by products such as MailChimp (**www.mailchimp.com**) AWeber Communications (**www.aweber.com**) or iContact (**www.icontact.com**).

# KEEP THE BUSINESS IN BALANCE

As the business continues to grow, you will want to maintain momentum and grow at a comfortable pace. Achieve this by following what I call 'the golden triangle', which will keep you and the business in balance. This requires spending roughly a third of your time on three key things:

## 1. Customer care

Look after your customers by delivering a quality product or service, on time and within budget. And remember ... the customer is always right!

I ask clients for feedback so that I can keep a check on what they're thinking and changes they'd like to see. It's good to know some personal details about your customers, too. (Maybe the date of their birthday, their favourite hobby or names of their children.) As you gather these details, make a quick note so that you can send a birthday card on the right date, enquire after GCSE results at the right time, etc. Don't go overboard, but showing that you care certainly won't harm your relationship.

Offer customers good service, regular communication and an innovative line of products and services. It will stand you in good stead.

## 2. New business

Taking care of customers means taking care of sales. Why? Because it costs less to win business from existing customers than it does to find new ones. And if customers are happy, they'll say good things about you to new and potential customers. This is called word-of-mouth marketing and achieving it is every business owner's dream!

Secure new clients through marketing, encouraging recommendations and direct-sales calls and pitches.

## 3. Admin

Not as enjoyable as the first two, but it still has to be done. Keep the books in order by raising invoices in good time, being on top of cash flow and filing tax returns and company documents on time and in order. In short, keep the finances in check and the books up-to-date.

# CASH IS KING

Keep an eye on the accounts so you can see how much money is in the bank, how much is owed and whether this covers your outgoings.

## Invoices

Be on time with invoicing and keep a record of amounts outstanding. I have a simple spreadsheet with five columns labelled 'client', 'invoice amount', 'invoice number', 'date submitted' and 'date paid'.

Your invoices should be a simple document with basic but thorough details. The less cause for question on the invoice, the faster it will be paid!

Settle invoices as promptly as you can but make use of the credit extended to you. Your suppliers will be grateful and should repay you with good service.

You can balance the budget with a piece of accounting software. Priced at between £50 and £100 for 'starter' versions, these packages offer sales and expense tracking, invoice templates, bank reconciliations and basic bookkeeping.

## Receipts

Keep business-related receipts in a place where they're easy to find. I have a big wicker box that doubles as a collecting place for receipts. It's helpful that they're all in one place when it's time to do the VAT return.

Denise Charlesworth-Smith is reaping the rewards of good planning and effective time management in her business . . .

# MONEY MAKER

**NAME**: Denise Charlesworth-Smith

**TALENT**: Jewellery

**BUSINESS**: Crystal Pig Accessories

DENISE CHARLESWORTH-SMITH'S jewellery business came about after being made redundant in 2008 from a career in project management, working for banks, insurance and latterly the police, hence the twist on the name, Crystal Pig Accessories.

"I love jewellery and decided to go on a course to learn how to make it – when I came home I could not wait to keep going, I was hooked!"

Denise's first sale came from a school craft fair before she decided to concentrate her efforts on wedding fairs.

"I can even remember the piece I sold, which was to a teacher at the school; it was a brooch which I turned into a fancy designed necklace and I'd really wanted to keep for myself!"

Denise's move into the wedding business came when she helped a bride whose wedding dress shop had gone into liquidation.

"Through this my first stockist got in touch and I'm now stocked in seven shops and outlets across the UK."

In terms of promotion, Denise finds word of mouth particularly effective, as well as social networking sites such as Facebook and Twitter.

"I try to encourage my customers to send me pictures of them wearing their Crystal Pig Accessories and I share these on Facebook. People then comment on them and this often leads to a sale. I have a number of regular clients who having bought a piece for their wedding are now fans and buyers of my designs."

Another avenue that has helped Crystal Pig Accessories was being featured in *PRIMA* magazine, which led to Denise teaching groups of young ladies and their mums in the school holidays, and she finds this great fun!

"The best form of promotion, though, is definitely recommendations from satisfied customers and of course showing off and wearing your designs and being asked 'where did you get that from?' I am lucky that I now have several outlets that regularly use my stock in photoshoots and we're also now going global due to pieces being bought from Europe and Australia."

The next twelve months are set to be busy for Denise.

"I've been approached to design a piece to go with a dress called the Grace Kelly design to be launched at the September bridal exhibition in Harrogate, so what with keeping up with orders and adding some extra lines to the business this year is going to be really busy! It has taken time but I now find that I am invited to showcase my designs at many prestigious fairs where before I found myself fighting to get in the door. My calendar is now organised so I can plan ahead. Now I see people copying my designs, but I'm flattered as I know that the originals have already hit the market two or more seasons before!"

Denise has learnt fast about running a business and the need to plan and be organised.

> "I've realised it's not all about adding beads to wires but working out a clear pricing structure, putting negotiating skills to good use and keeping ahead of the competition. I have also worked out how much is needed for things like advertising and marketing, training and materials in order to balance the books and pay the bills."

This planning and organisation has paid off, with Denise's most recent achievement being the opening of a studio to showcase designs and open up to private appointments. This is the latest development in a business that's set to keep on going and growing.

**TOP TIP!** *"Plan! Starting your own business is great but you need to plan, know what your own outlays are, be able to organise and juggle and also be flexible!"*

❀ **www.crystalpigaccessories.co.uk**

❀ **@CrystalPig**

# CHAPTER EIGHT
# GROWING THE
# BUSINESS

**Y**our business is getting known and making money and you're looking at options on how to scale and grow. Achieve this through:

❀ Product-ising

❀ Going global

❀ Outsourcing

# PRODUCT-ISING

If you're making handmade goods, you'll have soon realised there's only one of you and you can sell only as much as you can make! As scientists haven't yet worked out how to make more of you, in order to grow the business take the knowledge/skill/talent you have and put it in a box!

## KITS

Let's take the example of someone making unique dresses for girls; continue to make your signature style dress that is made by your own hands and at a price to reflect your time and dedication, but consider adding to the range with a dress kit that can be bought complete with material and clear instructions so parents can enjoy the experience of buying the kit and making their own dress whilst you enjoy selling more products (admittedly at a lower price) that have not taken as long to produce. At the end of the instructions you could also include details of where people can upload pictures of their creations to your blog or website, creating a sense of community and expanding the reach of your brand.

Julie Dodsworth has grown her business through a slightly different route in the form of licensing but it's a route that's proven successful . . .

# MONEY MAKER

**NAME**: Julie Dodsworth

**TALENT**: Design

**BUSINESS**: Julie Dodsworth

JULIE DODSWORTH's business is based around licensing her unique art.

> "It is a less usual route to market, and I had no experience or guidance in licensing and indeed no training or tuition in design but I had a belief, the encouragement of my family and a clear goal. Most of all I think it was just sheer perseverance that brought my dream to life."

Julie's dream began back in 2007 when she and her husband bought a narrow boat. Having built up a successful plant business in York, the couple were looking for a home-from-home in the South. Over the next couple of years, Julie began the personal hobby project of decorating their boat Calamity Jane.

> "I taught myself the folk art of canal painting, I adopted an 18th century style using primitive methods and painting outdoors. A vintage and folksy look became my style."

Not long after, Julie's daughter Bethany suggested the patterns she created could look nice on homeware items and the seed was sown. Julie visited a local garden centre and soon realised many of the familiar and successful high street brand names we all know are often manufactured by other, less well-known names.

> "I pieced together a matrix to find who exactly was behind those brand names and who were the elite of British production. From this, I researched who were the decision makers within manufacturing and started to promote myself to them."

It didn't take long for Julie to realise her single voice was being crowded out in the market.

"It was very much like singing on the street corner and trying to get a part in the West End! Each manufacturer has their own household name licensed brands, a portfolio of freelance artists they can call upon plus their own in-house designers. It's a mountain to climb."

However, in the spring of 2011, Julie's perseverance paid off as she launched her first textile ranges in 'Floral Romance' and 'Calamity Jane' with McCaw Allan, a textile company in Northern Ireland. From there Julie began to seek out more licenses and in 2012 had ten launched with more planned in the future. These include designs for textiles, candles, ceramics, stationery, gift-wrap and more.

Julie mostly works alone, with the help of Bethany whenever she needs it, and her business has already expanded overseas, in a big way: "My ranges now sell in over 500 shops and in seven countries."

Her advice to anyone else thinking of following in her footsteps is simple; don't give up, set yourself goals and reward yourself when you reach them, protect your art and most of all, enjoy it!

"I hold on to the absolute unbelievable magic of how it feels when you see your designs on the high street. Just amazing...and for me, all my dreams come true."

**TOP TIP!** *"If you never ask the question the answer will always be no!"*

❀ **www.juliedodsworth.co.uk**

❀ **www.facebook.com/julie.dodsworth.3**

# COURSES

Maybe you're selling works of art or making jam and want to productise – in which case, how about launching and teaching a class as an ideal way to expand? You get to meet customers and have an opportunity to talk to the press/promote classes in the media and have your name and brand appear in front of more people. You can even sell your produce at the classes!

When it comes to looking for space for such a class, consider your own home or approach the owner of the local coffee shop to ask if he/she would be happy for you to use the space at times when they are usually quiet; that way you're likely to get space for free in return for introducing footfall. Other places to consider could be your library, community centre/church hall or even a local business.

Laura Helps has decided to take the 'deliver training and classes' route to grow her cake-making (and now cake-make teaching) business . . .

# MONEY MAKER

**NAME**: Laura Helps

**TALENT**: Baking

**BUSINESS**: Cakes by Laura

LAURA HELPS began her cake business in 2008 after making a few cakes for friends and family.

"At the time, cake making wasn't as popular as it is now! I started by making bespoke cakes for clients, then expanded into selling equipment, and finally running cake-making workshops and parties, which form the bulk of my business now."

The business has since expanded into cupcake, cookie and cake-decorating classes, as well as a 'Starting your own Cake Making business' course which is proving very popular!

Laura's Cakes has expanded by using a range of different channels to promote the business and Laura thinks word of mouth is a key promotional tool.

"Word of mouth is the best and I also hand out my Moo cards to everyone I meet – they've all got pictures of my cakes on. My website is a promotion tool – in 2010, I paid a designer to develop a professional website and I think it really helps to separate me from my competition. I also use Facebook and Twitter to engage directly with people."

For Laura, quality is one of the things that keeps customers coming back.

"I try to offer quality cakes at the best price and I am now seeing the benefits as many of my customers are returning ones! With my cake decoration classes, sugarcraft is

addictive, so it's not too hard to attract students back! I also try and make my classes very informal and inexpensive, so people are more relaxed and feel they can recreate the products at home."

Over the next 12 months, Laura is looking to grow the business: "I'd love to have a shopfront. I currently have a premises but this is for classes only. I'm also getting married, so I'm planning to make the biggest and best wedding cake ever!"

**TOP TIP!** *"Research heavily whatever you're planning to do – talk to whoever you can. My friends and family are my greatest critics – they tell me if they think my newest bright idea is a terrible one. If you do come up with a brilliant idea, though, go for it...it's only a matter of time before someone else does!"*

❀ www.cakesbylaura.co.uk

❀ www.facebook.com/cakesbylaurauk

❀ @cakesbylaura

Once you have a space, let people know about the classes. Promote it on your website or blog, include a note in packages sent out, write a release/blog post for the media and local business sites, and make the most of local noticeboards, etc. Provide contact details so people can get in touch for more information and to book, and there you have it – you've set up an income-earning and brand-extending class!

# GOING GLOBAL

With exchange rates in our favour and enabling technology to hand, there's never been a better time to look beyond domestic shores for business. By virtue of having a professional window to the world (your website), start-ups and small businesses are going global faster than ever before.

In another of my books, *Go Global: How to take your business to the world,* I show how you can increase trade and broaden horizons in five simple steps. You will also find a free *Go Global* eBook on Enterprise Nation and a downloadable app – all the tools you need to be running an internationally successful business!

# OUTSOURCING

Grow profits by focusing on what you do best and outsourcing the rest. It's perfectly possible to achieve this and manage an expanding team from your own small office/home office.

## TEAMWORK SAVES TIME

The business is growing, time is your most precious resource and you are in need of help. The quickest and most affordable place to get it is from other companies with whom you can partner to get projects done, as well as from accredited advisors who will offer advice on how the business can continue to grow.

With outsourcing you can free yourself up to dedicate your attention to sales, strategy or whatever the business activity is that you do best. My advice to all businesses is always: focus on what you do best and outsource the rest.

## WHAT CAN BE OUTSOURCED, AND TO WHOM?

### Admin

Hire a VA (virtual assistant) to do the admin tasks you don't want or don't have the time to do. Visit VA directories and resources to find your perfect match.

❀ International Association of Virtual Assistants | **www.iava.org.uk**

❀ Society of Virtual Assistants | **www.societyofvirtualassistants.co.uk**

❀ Time Etc | **www.timeetc.co.uk**

❀ VA Success Group | **www.vasuccessgroup.co.uk**

❀ Administrative Consultants Association |
**www.administrativeconsultantsassoc.com**

❀ Virtual Assistant Coaching & Training Company | **www.vact.co.uk**

## PR, marketing and design

Outsource your PR to a specialist who can be pitching and promoting the business whilst you're at work. Find skilled professionals on directory sites such as Enterprise Nation and Business Smiths or contact companies such as PrPro, Press For Attention and Just In Time PR.

❀ Enterprise Nation | **www.enterprisenation.com**

❀ Business Smiths | **www.businesssmiths.co.uk**

❀ PrPro | **www.prpro.co.uk**

❀ Press For Attention PR | **www.pressforattention.com**

❀ Just In Time PR | **www.justintimepr.com**

## Sales

Hire a sales expert to make calls, set up appointments and attend trade shows. Find these professionals on Enterprise Nation (**www.enterprisenation.com**), contact telemarketing companies that offer outbound sales calls as a service, or look at sales specialists such as Inside and professionals like Jackie Wade.

❀ Great Guns | **www.greatgunsmarketing.co.uk**

❀ Inside | **www.theinsideteam.co.uk**

❀ Winning Sales | **www.winningsales.co.uk**

## Customer service

Looking after your customers is vital, but even that can be outsourced to great effect. Get Satisfaction's tagline is "people-powered customer service" – it provides a web-hosted platform, much like a forum, where customers can ask questions, suggest improvements, report a problem or give praise. It can save you time and money by making customer service an open process that leverages the wisdom of crowds. Questions are answered by other users, rather than you as the site host. You don't want to outsource this completely as it's good to show personal contact with customers, but this is a useful tool that could improve your business as customers offer their feedback.

❀ **www.getsatisfaction.com**

## IT

Spending too many hours trying to fix a single IT problem? Outsource the hassle and save your time, money and blood pressure. Find IT professionals on Enterprise Nation or contact IT support teams connected to the large retailers.

❀ Geeks-on-Wheels | **www.geeks-on-wheels.com**

❀ KnowHow | **www.knowhow.com**

❀ Geek Squad | **www.geeksquad.co.uk**

## Accounts

Unless you are in the accountancy business, this is almost a must to be outsourced. Monthly payroll, accounts, VAT returns and corporate tax returns all take time and it's time you can't afford or simply don't have. A cost/benefit analysis is likely to show that it's cheaper to outsource to a qualified accountant. Ask around for recommendations of accountants in your area who deliver a quality service at a competitive cost and are registered with the Institute of Chartered Accountants in England and Wales.

For online accounting and invoicing that makes life easier for you and your accountant, check out:

❈  FreeAgent | **www.freeagent.com**

❈  KashFlow | **www.kashflow.com**

❈  QuickBooks | **www.quickbooks.co.uk**

❈  Sage One | **www.sageone.com/accounts**

---

**TIP: HELP FROM AN ENTERN**

*If you have a project requiring specialist skill or attention consider hiring an entern –
an enthusiastic student or graduate who is passionate about entrepreneurship and
looking for work experience in young start-up companies.*

❈  **www.enternships.com**

---

Sandra Lewis has seen the benefit of teamwork at first-hand in launching and growing her business, following a successful corporate career . . .

# MONEY MAKER

**NAME**: Sandra Lewis

**TALENT**: Professional Virtual Services

**BUSINESS**: Worldwide101 Ltd

SANDRA LEWIS worked for over twenty years for companies such as Regus, with a focus on supporting small businesses to be effective as they scale. She travelled extensively to Asia, Australia, North America and in various parts of both Eastern and Western Europe, but decided in 2009 that she wanted to find a way to work globally from the comfort of her own home!

The idea of a virtual assistant business came to mind and shortly afterwards Worldwide101 was born.

> "Worldwide101 started off with just me providing services to entrepreneurs and small businesses, but over the months and years we have grown to a team of twelve virtual assistants located and working virtually on four continents supporting clients globally. We provide personalised virtual support, which means that we assign a dedicated team member who just happens to be half a world away."

Sandra spends much of her time promoting the business by writing articles for blogs and magazines, and also commenting on other pieces to give tips or provide information on remote working. "I have found that it's the best way to network, to get to know others with the same interest and ultimately dialogue about Worldwide101's services." One of Sandra's goals is to let people know about virtual support and how it can help their business.

Worldwide101 has found offering recurring services is a great way to keep customers engaged.

> "We practice upselling with our existing customers by suggesting other ways we might help – this has proven to be very successful and helpful to our clients as well (many times when a client is busy they don't know what they don't know/need!)"

Part of this success is the great team that Sandra has built around her, which now comprises of a team of virtual professionals located around the world.

> "The success of Worldwide101 is its people – we take great care to interview, test, review, etc. our team before hiring them."

The team's mission for the future is to provide admin and customer support no matter where their clients are located.

> "Virtual professional services are just getting started. Right now, there are still many businesses, start-ups and entrepreneurs who are unaware of the great benefits of hiring virtually and how easy it can be."

Sandra and her team are set to change this as they promote their message and business across borders.

## TOP TIPS!

**1.** *Do your homework – it's not enough to have a great idea. Make sure it's viable, practical and useful.*

**2.** *Stay focused – Success doesn't happen overnight. It takes effort, focus and perseverance to create something great.*

**3**. *Keep the company of those who believe in you – when it gets hard galvanise your friends and well-wishers so they can encourage you and remind you of why you started this in the first place!*

❀  **www.worldwide101.com**

❀  **www.facebook.com/worldwide101**

❀  **@BestVirtualHelp**

# FORM PARTNERSHIPS

If relationships with other companies and self-employed professionals develop you may decide to form a partnership. Consider writing a partnership agreement as your 'pre-nup' in business. At the outset of a relationship, all is good and you're excited about the potential, but it's best to be safe; have a few things written and agreed so all parties are clear on expectations.

The following should not be taken as concrete legal advice, more of a guideline on how to draw up an agreement. An agreement need only be a single page and cover the basics:

## Scope of agreement

What is your partnership working to achieve? For example, "This agreement is made between Company A and Company B. The agreement is related to the generation of online advertising revenues/hosting of an event/development of a new product."

### Respective responsibilities

Set out the expectations for who does what. For example, Company A will be responsible for promotion and business development and Company B will take on technical development and client care. Also include a note of how you'll keep each other briefed, maybe through the use of an online project management tool such as Basecamp.

### Finances

What will be the split in revenue, and is this before or after costs? Who owns the intellectual property? Consider including a clause that states the agreement will be reviewed in six months so that both parties can check on progress and have the right to cease the agreement if it hasn't gone as planned.

### Be fair

Agreements where both parties feel they're receiving their fair share are likely to be longer-lasting than those when one party feels embittered. Talk about this before writing and concluding the agreement. Make sure there's no resentment or sense of being exploited on either side.

### Sign it!

After making the effort to produce an agreement, be sure to both sign it! And then store it so you can access it easily if the need arises.

When writing the clauses in your agreement, think about all the things that could go wrong and safeguard against them. It's a practical exercise and won't harm your newly formed business relationship but will get it off on a firm footing. If you're looking for a template agreement, check out the following sites:

❀ Clickdocs | **www.clickdocs.co.uk**

❀ Off to see my Lawyer | **www.offtoseemylawyer.com**

# SEEK HELP AND SUPPORT

As a tweet to me once said: "Asking for help does not make you weak, but it could make you a success." Ask questions at every opportunity; of your peers, of mentors and accredited business advisors. Here's where to find them.

## PEERS

Who better to turn to than those who are also going through the experience of starting and growing a business? Visit the sites below and join their active forums and communities of business owners who will be more than happy to help.

- ❀ BusinessZone | **www.businesszone.co.uk**
- ❀ Start Up Donut | **www.startupdonut.co.uk**
- ❀ Enterprise Nation | **www.enterprisenation.com**

## MENTORS

The coalition government has announced a national mentoring programme and the recruitment of no less than 40,000 mentors who will be on hand to help young and start-up businesses.

- ❀ Mentorsme | **www.mentorsme.co.uk**

Over the ten-years-plus of running my own business, I have developed a view on mentors. It may not be a view with which you agree, as each business owner is different. But this is what has worked for me.

Don't restrict yourself to one mentor! I have learnt from many people as my businesses have passed through different stages of development. I would approach the person I felt best placed to have the answer, take on board their views, consider my options, and then act.

The ideal mentor is someone who possesses four things:

**1.** experience of your industry/sector

**2.** the ability to listen

**3.** the technical skills to advise

**4.** a willingness to make introductions to useful contacts.

If you can find these in one person, you are very fortunate. One of the finest things a mentor can do is allow you to talk. By doing so, you will often find you work out the answer. You sometimes just need a sounding board to answer your own question.

## ACCREDITED ADVISORS

When starting and growing your business, consider approaching your local enterprise agency for support. The National Enterprise Network acts as an umbrella organisation for all agencies. Local business advisors can help with everything from business planning to applying for funds and financial forecasting.

 **www.nationalenterprisenetwork.co.uk**

## STARTUP BRITAIN

In March 2011, a national campaign was launched to encourage more people to start a business and support existing businesses to grow. The campaign is run by a team of eight business owners and entrepreneurs, with support from the government and a number of corporate sponsors.

The face of the campaign is a website which offers links to useful resources and content, as well as valuable offers from large corporates and leading brands. Visit the site to be inspired and to celebrate the start-ups of Britain.

❀  **www.startupbritain.org**

## ENTERPRISE NATION

Turn to Enterprise Nation as your central resource and friend in business. Every month we:

❀  profile small business success stories

❀  release eBooks on topics that matter most

❀  produce videos with bite-size business advice

❀  host webchats with experts and special guests

❀  develop new tools to help you increase sales and reduce costs

❀  connect you to peers via friendly forums and social media.

Enterprise Nation is the place where you can access advice and support, raise profile and make sales.

❀  **www.enterprisenation.com** | **@e_nation**

# CONCLUSION

**I** hope this guide has offered all the tips and techniques you need to get going and growing!

With the information in hand and inspired by the stories of those who have started and succeeded, may I wish you well for what is sure to be an exciting and entrepreneurial adventure!

*Emma Jones*

**emma@enterprisenation.com | @emmaljones**

# MAKING A *LIVING* FROM WHAT YOU *LOVE*

*Whatever your passion, turn it into a way of life with these* Country Living *Magazine books ...*

**COOK WRAP SELL • DESIGN GROW SELL • DESIGN CREATE SELL**
**• TURN YOUR TALENT INTO A BUSINESS**
*www.brightwordpublishing.com*